AN EXPOSITION ON THE ORTHODOX FAITH

St. John of Damascus

Translated by: E.W. Watson, L. Pullan
Edited by: D.P. Curtin

Dalcassian
Publishing
Company
PHILADELPHIA, PA

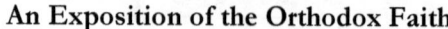

Library of Congress Cataloging-in-Publication Data

Copyright © 2018 Dalcassian Publishing Co.
In association with St. Macartan Press
All rights reserved.

BOOK I

Chapter 1. That the Deity is incomprehensible, and that we ought not to pry into and meddle with the things which have not been delivered to us by the holy Prophets, and Apostles, and Evangelists.

No one has seen God at any time; the Only-begotten Son, which is in the bosom of the Father, He has declared Him. The Deity, therefore, is ineffable and incomprehensible. *For no one knows the Father, save the Son, nor the Son, save the Father.* Matthew 11:27 And the Holy Spirit, too, so knows the things of God as the spirit of the man knows the things that are in him. 1 Corinthians 2:11 Moreover, after the first and blessed nature no one, not of men only, but even of supramundane powers, and the Cherubim, I say, and Seraphim themselves, has ever known God, save he to whom He revealed Himself.

God, however, did not leave us in absolute ignorance. For the knowledge of God's existence has been implanted by Him in all by nature. This creation, too, and its maintenance, and its government, proclaim the majesty of the Divine nature. Wisdom 13:5 Moreover, by the Law and the Prophets in former times and afterwards by His Only-begotten Son, our Lord and God and Saviour Jesus Christ, He disclosed to us the knowledge of Himself as that was possible for us. All things, therefore, that have been delivered to us by Law and Prophets and Apostles and Evangelists we receive, and know, and honour , seeking for nothing beyond these. For God, being good, is the cause of all good, subject neither to envy nor to any passion. For envy is far removed from the Divine nature, which is both passionless and only good. As knowing all things, therefore, and providing for what is profitable for each, He revealed that which it was to our profit to know; but what we were unable to bear He kept secret. With these things let us be satisfied, and let us abide by them, not removing everlasting boundaries, nor overpassing the divine tradition Proverbs 22:28 .

Chapter 2. Concerning things utterable and things unutterable, and things knowable and thing unknowable.

It is necessary, therefore, that one who wishes to speak or to hear of God should understand clearly that alike in the doctrine of Deity and in that of the Incarnation, neither are all things unutterable nor all utterable; neither all unknowable nor all knowable. But the knowable belongs to one order, and the utterable to another; just as it is one thing to speak and another thing to know. Many of the things relating to God, therefore, that are dimly understood cannot be put into fitting terms, but on things above us we cannot do else than express ourselves according to our limited capacity; as, for instance, when we speak of God we use the terms *sleep*, and *wrath*, and *regardlessness, hands*, too, and *feet*, and such like expressions.

We, therefore, both know and confess that God is without beginning, without end, eternal and everlasting, uncreate, unchangeable, invariable, simple, uncompound, incorporeal, invisible, impalpable, uncircumscribed, infinite, incognisable, indefinable, incomprehensible, good, just, maker of all things created, almighty, all-ruling, all-surveying, of all overseer, sovereign, judge; and that God is One, that is to say, one essence ; and that He is known , and has His being in three subsistences, in Father, I say, and Son and Holy Spirit; and that the Father and the Son and the Holy Spirit are one in all respects, except in that of not being begotten, that of being begotten, and that of procession; and that the Only-begotten Son and Word of God and God, in His bowels of mercy, for our salvation, by the good pleasure of God and the co-operation of the Holy Spirit, being conceived without seed, was born uncorruptedly of the Holy Virgin and Mother of God, Mary, by the Holy Spirit, and became of her perfect Man; and that the Same is at once perfect God and perfect Man, of two natures, Godhead and Manhood, and in two natures possessing intelligence, will and energy, and freedom, and, in a word, perfect according to the measure and proportion proper to each, at once to the divinity, I say, and to the humanity, yet to one composite person ; and that He suffered hunger and thirst and weariness, and was crucified, and for three days submitted to the experience of death and burial, and ascended to heaven, from which also He came to us, and shall come again. And the Holy Scripture is witness to this and the whole choir of the Saints.

But neither do we know, nor can we tell, what the essence of God is, or how it is in all, or how the Only-begotten Son and God, having emptied Himself, became Man of virgin blood, made by another law contrary to nature, or how He walked with dry feet upon the waters. It is not within our capacity, therefore, to say anything about God or even to think of Him, beyond the things which have been divinely revealed to us, whether by word or by manifestation, by the divine oracles at once of the Old Testament and of the New.

Chapter 3. Proof that there is a God.

That there is a God, then, is no matter of doubt to those who receive the Holy Scriptures, the Old Testament, I mean, and the New; nor indeed to most of the Greeks. For, as we said , the knowledge of the existence of God is implanted in us by nature. But since the wickedness of the Evil One has prevailed so mightily against man's nature as even to drive some into denying the existence of God, that most foolish and woe-fulest pit of destruction (whose folly David, revealer of the Divine meaning, exposed when he said , *The fool said in his heart, There is no God*), so the disciples of the Lord and His Apostles, made wise by the Holy Spirit and working wonders in His power and grace, took them captive in the net of miracles and drew them up out of the depths of ignorance to the light of the knowledge of God. In like manner also their successors in grace and worth, both pastors and teachers, having received the enlightening grace of the Spirit, were wont, alike by the power of miracles and the word of grace, to enlighten those walking in darkness and to bring back the wanderers into the way. But as for us who are not recipients either of the gift of miracles or the gift of teaching (for indeed we have rendered ourselves unworthy of these by our passion for pleasure), come, let us in connection with this theme discuss a few of those things which have been delivered to us on this subject by the expounders of grace, calling on the Father, the Son, and the Holy Spirit.

All things, that exist, are either created or uncreated. If, then, things are created, it follows that they are also wholly mutable. For things, whose existence originated in change, must also be subject to change, whether it be that they perish or that they become other than they are by act of will. But if things are uncreated they must in all consistency be also wholly immutable. For things which are opposed in the nature of their existence must also be opposed in the mode of their existence, that is to say, must have opposite properties: who, then, will refuse to grant that all existing things, not only such as come within the province of the senses, but even the very angels, are subject to change and transformation and movement of various kinds? For the things appertaining to the rational world, I mean angels and spirits and demons, are subject to changes of will, whether it is a progression or a retrogression in goodness, whether a struggle or a surrender; while the others suffer changes of generation and destruction, of increase and decrease, of quality and of movement in space. Things then that are mutable are also wholly created. But things that are created must be the work of some maker, and the maker cannot have been created. For if he had been created, he also must surely have been created by some one, and so on till we arrive at something uncreated. The Creator, then, being uncreated, is also wholly immutable. And what could this be other than Deity?

And even the very continuity of the creation, and its preservation and government, teach us that there does exist a Deity, who supports and maintains and preserves and ever provides for this universe. For how could opposite natures, such as fire and water, air and earth, have combined with each other so as to form one complete world, and continue to abide in indissoluble union, were there not some omnipotent power which bound them together and always is preserving them from dissolution?

What is it that gave order to things of heaven and things of earth, and all those things that move in the air and in the water, or rather to what was in existence before these, viz., to heaven and earth and air and the elements of fire and water? What was it that mingled and distributed these? What was it that set these in motion and keeps them in their unceasing and unhindered course ? Was it not the Artificer of these things, and He Who has implanted in everything the law whereby the universe is carried on and directed? Who then is the Artificer of these things? Is it not He Who created them and brought them into existence. For we shall not attribute such a power to the spontaneous. For, supposing their coming into existence was due to the spontaneous; what of the power that put all in order ? And let us grant this, if you please. What of that which has preserved and kept them in harmony with the original laws of their existence ? Clearly it is something quite distinct from the spontaneous. And what could this be other than Deity ?

Chapter 4. Concerning the nature of Deity: that it is incomprehensible.

It is plain, then, that there is a God. But what He is in His essence and nature is absolutely incomprehensible and unknowable. For it is evident that He is incorporeal. For how could that possess body which is infinite, and boundless, and formless, and intangible and invisible, in short, simple and not compound? How could that be immutable which is circumscribed and subject to passion? And how could that be passionless which is composed of elements and is resolved again into them? For combination is the beginning of conflict, and conflict of separation, and separation of dissolution, and dissolution is altogether foreign to God.

8

Again, how will it also be maintained that God permeates and fills the universe? As the Scriptures say, *Do not I fill heaven and earth, says the Lord* Jeremiah 23:24? For it is an impossibility that one body should permeate other bodies without dividing and being divided, and without being enveloped and contrasted, in the same way as all fluids mix and commingle.

But if some say that the body is immaterial, in the same way as the fifth body of which the Greek philosophers speak (which body is an impossibility), it will be wholly subject to motion like the heaven. For that is what they mean by the fifth body. Who then is it that moves it? For everything that is moved is moved by another thing. And who again is it that moves that? And so on to infinity till we at length arrive at something motionless. For the first mover is motionless, and that is the Deity. And must not that which is moved be circumscribed in space? The Deity, then, alone is motionless, moving the universe by immobility. So then it must be assumed that the Deity is incorporeal.

But even this gives no true idea of His essence, to say that He is unbegotten, and without beginning, changeless and imperishable, and possessed of such other qualities as we are wont to ascribe to God and His environment. For these do not indicate what He is, but what He is not. But when we would explain what the essence of anything is, we must not speak only negatively. In the case of God, however, it is impossible to explain what He is in His essence, and it befits us the rather to hold discourse about His absolute separation from all things. For He does not belong to the class of existing things: not that He has no existence , but that He is above all existing things, nay even above existence itself. For if all forms of knowledge have to do with what exists, assuredly that which is above knowledge must certainly be also above essence : and, conversely, that which is above essence will also be above knowledge.

God then is infinite and incomprehensible and all that is comprehensible about Him is His infinity and incomprehensibility. But all that we can affirm concerning God does not show forth God's nature, but only the qualities of His nature. For when you speak of Him as good, and just, and wise, and so forth, you do not tell God's nature but only the qualities of His nature. Further there are some affirmations which we make concerning God which have the force of absolute negation: for example, when we use the term darkness, in reference to God, we do not mean darkness itself, but that He is not light but above light: and when we speak of Him as light, we mean that He is not darkness.

Chapter 5. Proof that God is one and not many.

We have, then, adequately demonstrated that there is a God, and that His essence is incomprehensible. But that God is one and not many is no matter of doubt to those who believe in the Holy Scriptures. For the Lord says in the beginning of the Law: *I am the Lord your God, which have brought you out of the land of Egypt. You shall have no other Gods before Me.* Exodus 20:2-3 And again He says, *Hear, O Israel, the Lord our God is one Lord.* Deuteronomy 6:4 And in Isaiah the prophet we read, *For I am the first God and I am the last, and beside Me there is no God. Before Me there was not any God, nor after Me will there be any God, and beside Me there is no God.* Isaiah 43:10 And the Lord, too, in the holy gospels speaks these words to His Father, *And this is life eternal, that they may know You the only true God.* John 17:3 But with those that do not believe in the Holy Scriptures we will reason thus.

The Deity is perfect , and without blemish in goodness, and wisdom, and power, without beginning, without end, everlasting, uncircumscribed , and in short, perfect in all things. Should we say, then, that there are many Gods, we must recognise difference among the many. For if there is no difference among them, they are one rather than many. But if there is difference among them, what becomes of the perfectness? For that which comes short of perfection, whether it be in goodness, or power, or wisdom, or time, or place, could not be God. But it is this very identity in all respects that shows that the Deity is one and not many.

Again, if there are many Gods, how can one maintain that God is uncircumscribed? For where the one would be, the other could not be.

Further, how could the world be governed by many and saved from dissolution and destruction, while strife is seen to rage between the rulers? For difference introduces strife. And if any one should say that each rules over a part, what of that which established this order and gave to each his particular realm? For this would the rather be God. Therefore, God is one, perfect, uncircumscribed, maker of the universe, and its preserver and governor, exceeding and preceding all perfection.

Moreover, it is a natural necessity that duality should originate in unity.

Chapter 6. Concerning the Word and the Son of God: a reasoned proof.

So then this one and only God is not Wordless. And possessing the Word, He will have it not as without a subsistence, nor as having had a beginning, nor as destined to cease to be. For there never was a time when God was not Word: but He ever possesses His own Word, begotten of Himself, not, as our word is, without a subsistence and dissolving into air, but having a subsistence in Him and life and perfection, not proceeding out of Himself but ever existing within Himself. For where could it be, if it were to go outside Him? For inasmuch as our nature is perishable and easily dissolved, our word is also without subsistence. But since God is everlasting and perfect, He will have His Word subsistent in Him, and everlasting and living, and possessed of all the attributes of the Begetter. For just as our word, proceeding as it does out of the mind, is neither wholly identical with the mind nor utterly diverse from it (for so far as it proceeds out of the mind it is different from it, while so far as it reveals the mind, it is no longer absolutely diverse from the mind, but being one in nature with the mind, it is yet to the subject diverse from it), so in the same manner also the Word of God in its independent subsistence is differentiated from Him from Whom it derives its subsistence : but inasmuch as it displays in itself the same attributes as are seen in God, it is of the same nature as God. For just as absolute perfection is contemplated in the Father, so also is it contemplated in the Word that is begotten of Him.

Chapter 7. Concerning the Holy Spirit, a reasoned proof.

Moreover the Word must also possess Spirit. For in fact even our word is not destitute of spirit; but in our case the spirit is something different from our essence. For there is an attraction and movement of the air which is drawn in and poured forth that the body may be sustained. And it is this which in the moment of utterance becomes the articulate word, revealing in itself the force of the word. But in the case of the divine nature, which is simple and uncompound, we must confess in all piety that there exists a Spirit of God, for the Word is not more imperfect than our own word. Now we cannot, in piety, consider the Spirit to be something foreign that gains admission into God from without, as is the case with compound natures like us. Nay, just as, when we heard of the Word of God, we considered it to be not without subsistence, nor the product of learning, nor the mere utterance of voice, nor as passing into the air and perishing, but as being essentially subsisting, endowed with free volition, and energy, and omnipotence: so also, when we have learned about the Spirit of God, we contemplate it as the companion of the Word and the revealer of His energy, and not as mere breath without subsistence. For to conceive of the Spirit that dwells in God as after the likeness of our own spirit, would be to drag down the greatness of the divine nature to the lowest depths of degradation. But we must contemplate it as an essential power, existing in its own proper and peculiar subsistence, proceeding from the Father and resting in the Word , and showing forth the Word, neither capable of disjunction from God in Whom it exists, and the Word Whose companion it is, nor poured forth to vanish into nothingness , but being in subsistence in the likeness of the Word, endowed with life, free volition, independent movement, energy, ever willing that which is good, and having power to keep pace with the will in all its decrees , having no beginning and no end. For never was the Father at any time lacking in the Word, nor the Word in the Spirit.

Thus because of the unity in nature, the error of the Greeks in holding that God is many, is utterly destroyed: and again by our acceptance of the Word and the Spirit, the dogma of the Jews is overthrown: and there remains of each party only what is profitable. On the one hand of the Jewish idea we have the unity of God's nature, and on the other, of the Greek, we have the distinction in subsistences and that only.

But should the Jew refuse to accept the Word and the Spirit, let the divine Scripture confute him and curb his tongue. For concerning the Word, the divine David says, *For ever, O Lord, Your Word is settled in heaven.* And again, *He sent His Word and healed them.* But the word that is uttered is not sent, nor is it for ever settled. And concerning the Spirit, the same David says, *You send forth Your Spirit, they are created.* And again, *By the word of the Lord were the heavens made: and all the host of them by the breath of His mouth.* Job, too, says, *The Spirit of God has made me, and the breath of the Almighty has given me life.* Job 33:4 Now the Spirit which is sent and makes and establishes and conserves, is not mere breath that dissolves, any more than the mouth of God is a bodily member. For the conception of both must be such as harmonizes with the Divine nature.

Chapter 8. Concerning the Holy Trinity.

We believe, then, in One God, one beginning , having no beginning, uncreate, unbegotten, imperishable and immortal, everlasting, infinite, uncircumscribed, boundless, of infinite power, simple, uncompound, incorporeal, without flux, passionless, unchangeable, unalterable, unseen, the fountain of goodness and justice, the light of the mind, inaccessible; a power known by no measure, measurable only by His own will alone (for all things that He wills He can), creator of all created things, seen or unseen, of all the maintainer and preserver, for all the provider, master and lord and king over all, with an endless and immortal kingdom: having no contrary, filling all, by nothing encompassed, but rather Himself the encompasser and maintainer and original possessor of the universe, occupying all essences intact and extending beyond all things, and being separate from all essence as being super-essential and above all things and absolute God, absolute goodness, and absolute fullness : determining all sovereignties and ranks, being placed above all sovereignty and rank, above essence and life and word and thought: being Himself very light and goodness and life and essence, inasmuch as He does not derive His being from another, that is to say, of those things that exist: but being Himself the fountain of being to all that is, of life to the living, of reason to those that have reason; to all the cause of all good: perceiving all things even before they have become: one essence, one divinity, one power, one will, one energy, one beginning, one authority, one dominion, one sovereignty, made known in three perfect subsistences and adored with one adoration, believed in and ministered to by all rational creation , united without confusion and divided without separation (which indeed transcends thought). (We believe) in Father and Son and Holy Spirit whereinto also we have been baptized. For so our Lord commanded the Apostles to baptize, saying, *Baptizing them in the name of the Father, Son, and Holy Spirit* Matthew 18:19 .

(We believe) in one Father, the beginning , and cause of all: begotten of no one: without cause or generation, alone subsisting: creator of all: but Father of one only by nature, His Only-begotten Son and our Lord and God and Saviour Jesus Christ, and Producer of the most Holy Spirit. And in one Son of God, the Only-begotten, our Lord, Jesus Christ: begotten of the Father, before all the ages: Light of Light, true God of true God: begotten, not made, consubstantial with the Father, through Whom all things are made: and when we say He was before all the ages we show that His birth is without time or beginning: for the Son of God was not brought into being out of nothing , He that is the effulgence of the glory, the impress of the Father's subsistence , the living wisdom and power 1 Corinthians 1:24, the Word possessing interior subsistence , the essential and perfect and living image Hebrews 1:3 of the unseen God. But always He was with the Father and in Him , everlastingly and without beginning begotten of Him. For there never was a time when the Father was and the Son was not, but always the Father and always the Son, Who was begotten of Him, existed together. For He could not have received the name Father apart from the Son: for if He were without the Son , He could not be the Father: and if He thereafter had the Son, thereafter He became the Father, not having been the Father prior to this, and He was changed from that which was not the Father and became the Father. This is the worst form of blasphemy. For we may not speak of God as destitute of natural generative power: and generative power means, the power of producing from one's self, that is to say, from one's own proper essence, that which is like in nature to one's self.

In treating, then, of the generation of the Son, it is an act of impiety to say that time comes into play and that the existence of the Son is of later origin than the Father. For we hold that it is from Him, that is, from the Father's nature, that the Son is generated. And unless we grant that the Son co-existed from the beginning with the Father, by Whom He was begotten, we introduce change into the Father's subsistence, because, not being the Father, He subsequently became the Father. For the creation, even though it originated later, is nevertheless not derived from the essence of God, but is brought into existence out of nothing by His will and power, and change does not touch God's nature. For generation means that the begetter produces out of his essence offspring similar in essence. But creation and making mean that the creator and maker produces from that which is external, and not out of his own essence, a creation of an absolutely dissimilar nature.

Wherefore in God, Who alone is passionless and unalterable, and immutable, and ever so continues, both begetting and creating are passionless. For being by nature passionless and not liable to flux, since He is simple and uncompound, He is not subject to passion or flux either in begetting or in creating, nor has He need of any co-operation. But generation in Him is without beginning and everlasting, being the work of nature and producing out of His own essence, that the Begetter may not undergo change, and that He may not be God first and God last, nor receive any accession: while creation in the case of God , being the work of will, is not co-eternal with God. For it is not natural that that which is brought into existence out of nothing should be co-eternal with what is without beginning and everlasting. There is this difference in fact between man's making and God's. Man can bring nothing into existence out of nothing , but all that he makes requires pre-existing matter for its basis , and he does not create it by will only, but thinks out first what it is to be and pictures it in his mind, and only then fashions it with his hands, undergoing labour and trouble , and often missing the mark and failing to produce to his satisfaction that after which he strives. But God, through the exercise of will alone, has brought all things into existence out of nothing. Now there is the same difference between God and man in begetting and generating. For in God, Who is without time and beginning, passionless, not liable to flux, incorporeal, alone and without end , generation is without time and beginning, passionless and not liable to flux, nor dependent on the union of two : nor has His own incomprehensible generation beginning or end. And it is without beginning because He is immutable: without flux because He is passionless and incorporeal: independent of the union of two again because He is incorporeal but also because He is the one and only God, and stands in need of no co-operation: and without end or cessation because He is without beginning, or time, or end, and ever continues the same. For that which has no beginning has no end: but that which through grace is endless is assuredly not without beginning, as, witness, the angels.

Accordingly the everlasting God generates His own Word which is perfect, without beginning and without end, that God, Whose nature and existence are above time, may not engender in time. But with man clearly it is otherwise, for generation is with him a matter of sex, and destruction and flux and increase and body clothe him round about , and he possesses a nature which is male or female. For the male requires the assistance of the female. But may He Who surpasses all, and transcends all thought and comprehension, be gracious to us.

The holy catholic and apostolic Church, then, teaches the existence at once of a Father: and of His Only-begotten Son, born of Him without time and flux and passion, in a manner incomprehensible and perceived by the God of the universe alone: just as we recognise the existence at once of fire and the light which proceeds from it: for there is not first fire and thereafter light, but they exist together. And just as light is ever the product of fire, and ever is in it and at no time is separate from it, so in like manner also the Son is begotten of the Father and is never in any way separate from Him, but ever is in Him. But whereas the light which is produced from fire without separation, and abides ever in it, has no proper subsistence of its own distinct from that of fire (for it is a natural quality of fire), the Only-begotten Son of God, begotten of the Father without separation and difference and ever abiding in Him, has a proper subsistence of its own distinct from that of the Father.

The terms, 'Word' and 'effulgence,' then, are used because He is begotten of the Father without the union of two, or passion, or time, or flux, or separation : and the terms 'Son' and 'impress of the Father's subsistence,' because He is perfect and has subsistence and is in all respects similar to the Father, save that the Father is not begotten : and the term 'Only-begotten' because He alone was begotten alone of the Father alone. For no other generation is like to the generation of the Son of God, since no other is Son of God. For though the Holy Spirit proceeds from the Father, yet this is not generative in character but processional. This is a different mode of existence, alike incomprehensible and unknown, just as is the generation of the Son. Wherefore all the qualities the Father has are the Son's, save that the Father is unbegotten , and this exception involves no difference in essence nor dignity , but only a different mode of coming into existence. We have an analogy in Adam, who was not begotten (for God Himself moulded him), and Seth, who was begotten (for he is Adam's son), and Eve, who proceeded out of Adam's rib (for she was not begotten). These do not differ from each other in nature, for they are human beings: but they differ in the mode of coming into existence.

For one must recognise that the word ἀγένητον with only one 'ν ' signifies uncreate or not having been made, while ἀγέννητον written with double 'ν ' means unbegotten. According to the first significance essence differs from essence: for one essence is uncreate, or ἀγένητον with one 'ν,' and another is create or γενητή . But in the second significance there is no difference between essence and essence. For the first subsistence of all kinds of living creatures is ἀγέννητος but not ἀγένητος . For they were created by the Creator, being brought into being by His Word, but they were not begotten, for there was no pre-existing form like themselves from which they might have been born.

So then in the first sense of the word the three absolutely divine subsistences of the Holy Godhead agree : for they exist as one in essence and uncreate. But with the second signification it is quite otherwise. For the Father alone is ingenerate , no other subsistence having given Him being. And the Son alone is generate, for He was begotten of the Father's essence without beginning and without time. And only the Holy Spirit proceeds from the Father's essence, not having been generated but simply proceeding. John 15:26 For this is the doctrine of Holy Scripture. But the nature of the generation and the procession is quite beyond comprehension.

And this also it behooves us to know, that the names Fatherhood, Sonship and Procession, were not applied to the Holy Godhead by us: on the contrary, they were communicated to us by the Godhead, as the divine apostle says, *Wherefore I bow the knee to the Father, from Whom is every family in heaven and on earth.* But if we say that the Father is the origin of the Son and greater than the Son, we do not suggest any precedence in time or superiority in nature of the Father over the Son John 14:28 (for through His agency He made the ages), or superiority in any other respect save causation. And we mean by this, that the Son is begotten of the Father and not the Father of the Son, and that the Father naturally is the cause of the Son: just as we say in the same way not that fire proceeds from light, but rather light from fire. So then, whenever we hear it said that the Father is the origin of the Son and greater than the Son, let us understand it to mean in respect of causation. And just as we do not say that fire is of one essence and light of another, so we cannot say that the Father is of one essence and the Son of another: but both are of one and the same essence. And just as we say that fire has brightness through the light proceeding from it, and do not consider the light of the fire as an instrument ministering to the fire, but rather as its natural force: so we say that the Father creates all that He creates through His Only-begotten Son, not as though the Son were a mere instrument serving the Father's ends, but as His natural and subsistential force. And just as we say both that the fire shines and again that the light of the fire shines, *So all things whatsoever the Father does, these also does the Son likewise.* John 5:19 But whereas light possesses no proper subsistence of its own, distinct from that of the fire, the Son is a perfect subsistence , inseparable from the Father's subsistence, as we have shown above. For it is quite impossible to find in creation an image that will illustrate in itself exactly in all details the nature of the Holy Trinity. For how could that which is create and compound, subject to flux and change, circumscribed, formed and corruptible, clearly show forth the super-essential divine essence, unaffected as it is in any of these ways? Now it is evident that all creation is liable to most of these affections, and all from its very nature is subject to corruption.

Likewise we believe also in one Holy Spirit, the Lord and Giver of Life: Who proceeds from the Father and rests in the Son: the object of equal adoration and glorification with the Father and Son, since He is co-essential and co-eternal : the Spirit of God, direct, authoritative , the fountain of wisdom, and life, and holiness: God existing and addressed along with Father and Son: uncreate, full, creative, all-ruling, all-effecting, all-powerful, of infinite power, Lord of all creation and not under any lord : deifying, not deified : filling, not filled: shared in, not sharing in: sanctifying, not sanctified: the intercessor, receiving the supplications of all: in all things like to the Father and Son: proceeding from the Father and communicated through the Son, and participated in by all creation, through Himself creating, and investing with essence and sanctifying, and maintaining the universe: having subsistence, existing in its own proper and peculiar subsistence, inseparable and indivisible from Father and Son, and possessing all the qualities that the Father and Son possess, save that of not being begotten or born. For the Father is without cause and unborn: for He is derived from nothing, but derives from Himself His being, nor does He derive a single quality from another. Rather He is Himself the beginning and cause of the existence of all things in a definite and natural manner. But the Son is derived from the Father after the manner of generation, and the Holy Spirit likewise is derived from the Father, yet not after the manner of generation, but after that of procession. And we have learned that there is a difference between generation and procession, but the nature of that difference we in no wise understand. Further, the generation of the Son from the Father and the procession of the Holy Spirit are simultaneous.

All then that the Son and the Spirit have is from the Father, even their very being : and unless the Father is, neither the Son nor the Spirit is. And unless the Father possesses a certain attribute, neither the Son nor the Spirit possesses it: and through the Father , that is, because of the Father's existence , the Son and the Spirit exist , and through the Father, that is, because of the Father having the qualities, the Son and the Spirit have all their qualities, those of being unbegotten, and of birth and of procession being excepted. For in these *hypo static* or *personal* properties alone do the three holy subsistences differ from each other, being indivisibly divided not by essence but by the distinguishing mark of their proper and peculiar subsistence.

Further we say that each of the three has a perfect subsistence, that we may understand not one compound perfect nature made up of three imperfect elements, but one simple essence, surpassing and preceding perfection, existing in three perfect subsistences. For all that is composed of imperfect elements must necessarily be compound. But from perfect subsistences no compound can arise. Wherefore we do not speak of the form as from subsistences, but as in subsistences. But we speak of those things as imperfect which do not preserve the form of that which is completed out of them. For stone and wood and iron are each perfect in its own nature, but with reference to the building that is completed out of them each is imperfect: for none of them is in itself a house.

The subsistences then we say are perfect, that we may not conceive of the divine nature as compound. For compoundness is the beginning of separation. And again we speak of the three subsistences as being in each other , that we may not introduce a crowd and multitude of Gods. Owing to the three subsistences, there is no compoundness or confusion: while, owing to their having the same essence and dwelling in one another, and being the same in will, and energy, and power, and authority, and movement, so to speak, we recognise the indivisibility and the unity of God. For verily there is one God, and His word and Spirit.

Marg. ms. Concerning the distinction of the three subsistences: and concerning the thing itself and our reason and thought in relation to it.

One ought, moreover, to recognise that it is one thing to look at a matter as it is, and another thing to look at it in the light of reason and thought. In the case of all created things, the distinction of the subsistences is observed in actual fact. For in actual fact Peter is seen to be separate from Paul. But the community and connection and unity are apprehended by reason and thought. For it is by the mind that we perceive that Peter and Paul are of the same nature and have one common nature. For both are living creatures, rational and mortal: and both are flesh, endowed with the spirit of reason and understanding. It is, then, by reason that this community of nature is observed. For here indeed the subsistences do not exist one within the other. But each privately and individually, that is to say, in itself, stands quite separate, having very many points that divide it from the other. For they are both separated in space and differ in time, and are divided in thought, and power, and shape, or form, and habit, and temperament and dignity, and pursuits, and all differentiating properties, but above all, in the fact that they do not dwell in one another but are separated. Hence it comes that we can speak of two, three, or many men.

And this may be perceived throughout the whole of creation, but in the case of the holy and superessential and incomprehensible Trinity, far removed from everything, it is quite the reverse. For there the community and unity are observed in fact, through the co-eternity of the subsistences, and through their having the same essence and energy and will and concord of mind , and then being identical in authority and power and goodness — I do not say similar but identical — and then movement by one impulse. For there is one essence, one goodness, one power, one will, one energy, one authority, one and the same, I repeat, not three resembling each other. But the three subsistences have one and the same movement. For each one of them is related as closely to the other as to itself: that is to say that the Father, the Son, and the Holy Spirit are one in all respects, save those of not being begotten, of birth and of procession. But it is by thought that the difference is perceived. For we recognise one God: but only in the attributes of Fatherhood, Sonship, and Procession, both in respect of cause and effect and perfection of subsistence, that is, manner of existence, do we perceive difference. For with reference to the uncircumscribed Deity we cannot speak of separation in space, as we can in our own case. For the subsistences dwell in one another, in no wise confused but cleaving together, according to the word of the Lord, *I am in the father, and the father in Me* John 14:11: nor can one admit difference in will or judgment or energy or power or anything else whatsoever which may produce actual and absolute separation in our case. Wherefore we do not speak of three Gods, the Father, the Son, and the Holy Spirit, but rather of one God, the holy Trinity, the Son and Spirit being referred to one cause , and not compounded or coalesced according to the synæresis of Sabellius. For, as we said, they are made one not so as to commingle, but so as to cleave to each other, and they have their being in each other without any coalescence or commingling. Nor do the Son and the Spirit stand apart, nor are they sundered in essence according to the diæresis of Arias. For the Deity is undivided among things divided, to put it concisely: and it is just like three suns cleaving to each other without separation and giving out light mingled and conjoined into one. When, then, we turn our eyes to the Divinity, and the first cause and the sovereignty and the oneness and sameness, so to speak, of the movement and will of the Divinity, and the identity in essence and power and energy and lordship, what is seen by us is unity. But when we look to those things in which the Divinity is, or, to put it more accurately, which are the Divinity, and those things which are in it through the first cause without time or distinction in glory or separation, that is to say, the subsistences of the Son and the Spirit, it seems to us a Trinity that we adore. The Father is one Father, and without beginning, that is, without cause: for He is not derived from anything. The Son is one Son, but not without beginning, that is, not without cause: for He is derived from the Father. But if you eliminate the idea of a beginning from time, He is also without beginning: for the creator of times cannot be subject to time. The Holy Spirit is one Spirit, going forth from the Father, not in the manner of Sonship but of procession; so that neither has the Father lost His property of being unbegotten because He has begotten, nor has the Son lost His property of being begotten because He was begotten of that which was unbegotten (for how could that be so?), nor does the Spirit change either into the Father or into the Son because He has proceeded and is God. For a property is quite constant. For how could a property persist if it were variable, moveable, and could change into something else? For if the Father is the Son, He is not strictly the Father: for there is strictly one Father. And if the Son is the Father, He is not strictly the Son: for there is strictly one Son and one Holy Spirit.

Further, it should be understood that we do not speak of the Father as derived from any one, but we speak of Him as the Father of the Son. And we do not speak of the Son as Cause or Father, but we speak of Him both as from the Father, and as the Son of the Father. And we speak likewise of the Holy Spirit as from the Father, and call Him the Spirit of the Father. And we do not speak of the Spirit as from the Son : but yet we call Him the Spirit of the Son. *For if any one has not the Spirit of Christ, he is none of His* Romans 8:9, says the divine apostle. And we confess that He is manifested and imparted to us through the Son. *For He breathed upon His Disciples, says he, and said, Receive the Holy Spirit.* John 20:29 It is just the same as in the case of the sun from which come both the ray and the radiance (for the sun itself is the source of both the ray and the radiance), and it is through the ray that the radiance is imparted to us, and it is the radiance itself by which we are lightened and in which we participate. Further we do not speak of the Son of the Spirit, or of the Son as derived from the Spirit.

Chapter 9. Concerning what is affirmed about God.

The Deity is simple and uncompound. But that which is composed of many and different elements is compound. If, then, we should speak of the qualities of being uncreate and without beginning and incorporeal and immortal and everlasting and good and creative and so forth as essential differences in the case of God, that which is composed of so many qualities will not be simple but must be compound. But this is impious in the extreme. Each then of the affirmations about God should be thought of as signifying not what He is in essence, but either something that it is impossible to make plain, or some relation to some of those things which are contrasts or some of those things that follow the nature, or an energy.

It appears then that the most proper of all the names given to God is He that is, as He Himself said in answer to Moses on the mountain, *Say to the sons of Israel, He that is has sent Me.* Exodus 3:14 For He keeps all being in His own embrace , like a sea of essence infinite and unseen. Or as the holy Dionysius says, He that is good. For one cannot say of God that He has being in the first place and goodness in the second.

The second name of God is ὁ Θεός, derived from θέειν , to run, because He courses through all things, or from αἴθειν, to burn: *For God is a fire consuming all evil* Deuteronomy 4:24: or from θεᾶσθαι, because He is all-seeing

2 Maccabees 10:5: for nothing can escape Him, and over all He keeps watch. For He saw all things before they were, holding them timelessly in His thoughts; and each one conformably to His voluntary and timeless thought , which constitutes predetermination and image and pattern, comes into existence at the predetermined time.

The first name then conveys the notion of His existence and of the nature of His existence: while the second contains the idea of energy. Further, the terms 'without beginning,' 'incorruptible,' 'unbegotten,' as also 'uncreate,' 'incorporeal,' 'unseen,' and so forth, explain what He is not: that is to say, they tell us that His being had no beginning, that He is not corruptible, nor created, nor corporeal, nor visible. Again, goodness and justice and piety and such like names belong to the nature , but do not explain His actual essence. Finally, Lord and King and names of that class indicate a relationship with their contrasts: for the name Lord has reference to those over whom the lord rules, and the name King to those under kingly authority, and the name Creator to the creatures, and the name Shepherd to the sheep he tends.

Chapter 10. Concerning divine union and separation.

Therefore all these names must be understood as common to deity as a whole, and as containing the notions of sameness and simplicity and indivisibility and union: while the names Father, Son and Spirit, and causeless and caused, and unbegotten and begotten, and procession contain the idea of separation: for these terms do not explain His essence, but the mutual relationship and manner of existence.

When, then, we have perceived these things and are conducted from these to the divine essence, we do not apprehend the essence itself but only the attributes of the essence: just as we have not apprehended the essence of the soul even when we have learned that it is incorporeal and without magnitude and form: nor again, the essence of the body when we know that it is white or black, but only the attributes of the essence. Further, the true doctrine teaches that the Deity is simple and has one simple energy, good and energising in all things, just as the sun's ray, which warms all things and energises in each in harmony with its natural aptitude and receptive power, having obtained this form of energy from God, its Maker.

But quite distinct is all that pertains to the divine and benignant incarnation of the divine Word. For in that neither the Father nor the Spirit have any part at all, unless so far as regards approval and the working of inexplicable miracles which the God-Word, having become man like us, worked, as unchangeable God and son of God.

Chapter 11. Concerning what is affirmed about God as though He had body.

Since we find many terms used symbolically in the Scriptures concerning God which are more applicable to that which has body, we should recognise that it is quite impossible for us men clothed about with this dense covering of flesh to understand or speak of the divine and lofty and immaterial energies of the Godhead, except by the use of images and types and symbols derived from our own life. So then all the statements concerning God, that imply body, are symbols, but have a higher meaning: for the Deity is simple and formless. Hence by God's eyes and eyelids and sight we are to understand His power of overseeing all things and His knowledge, that nothing can escape: for in the case of us this sense makes our knowledge more complete and more full of certainty. By God's ears and hearing is meant His readiness to be propitiated and to receive our petitions: for it is this sense that renders us also kind to suppliants, inclining our ear to them more graciously. God's mouth and speech are His means of indicating His will; for it is by the mouth and speech that we make clear the thoughts that are in the heart: God's food and drink are our concurrence to His will, for we, too, satisfy the necessities of our natural appetite through the sense of taste. And God's sense of smell is His appreciation of our thoughts of and good will towards Him, for it is through this sense that we appreciate sweet fragrance. And God's countenance is the demonstration and manifestation of Himself through His works, for our manifestation is through the countenance. And God's hands mean the effectual nature of His energy, for it is with our own hands that we accomplish our most useful and valuable work. And His right hand is His aid in prosperity, for it is the right hand that we also use when making anything of beautiful shape or of great value, or where much strength is required. His handling is His power of accurate discrimination and exaction, even in the minutest and most secret details, for those whom we have handled cannot conceal from us anything within themselves. His feet and walk are His advent and presence, either for the purpose of bringing succour to the needy, or vengeance against enemies, or to perform any other action, for it is by using our feet that we come to arrive at any place. His oath is the unchangeableness of His counsel, for it is by oath that we confirm our compacts with one another. His anger and fury are His hatred of and aversion to all wickedness, for we, too, hate that which is contrary to our mind and become enraged thereat. His forgetfulness and sleep and slumbering are His delay in taking vengeance on His enemies and the postponement of the accustomed help to His own. And to put it shortly, all the statements made about God that imply body have some hidden meaning and teach us what is above us by means of something familiar to ourselves, with the exception of any statement concerning the bodily sojourn of the God-Word. For He for our safety took upon Himself the whole nature of man , the thinking spirit, the body, and all the properties of human nature, even the natural and blameless passions.

Chapter 12. Concerning the Same.

The following, then, are the mysteries which we have learned from the holy oracles, as the divine Dionysius the Areopagite said : that God is the cause and beginning of all: the essence of all that have essence: the life of the living: the reason of all rational beings: the intellect of all intelligent beings: the recalling and restoring of those who fall away from Him: the renovation and transformation of those that corrupt that which is natural: the holy foundation of those who are tossed in unholiness: the steadfastness of those who have stood firm: the way of those whose course is directed to Him and the hand stretched forth to guide them upwards. And I shall add He is also the Father of all His creatures (for God, Who brought us into being out of nothing, is in a stricter sense our Father than are our parents who have derived both being and begetting from Him): the shepherd of those who follow and are tended by Him: the radiance of those who are enlightened: the initiation of the initiated: the deification of the deified: the peace of those at discord: the simplicity of those who love simplicity: the unity of those who worship unity: of all beginning the beginning, super-essential because above all beginning : and the good revelation of what is hidden, that is, of the knowledge of Him so far as that is lawful for and attainable by each.

Further and more accurately concerning divine names

The Deity being incomprehensible is also assuredly nameless. Therefore since we know not His essence, let us not seek for a name for His essence. For names are explanations of actual things. But God, Who is good and brought us out of nothing into being that we might share in His goodness, and Who gave us the faculty of knowledge, not only did not impart to us His essence, but did not even grant us the knowledge of His essence. For it is impossible for nature to understand fully the supernatural. Moreover, if knowledge is of things that are , how can there be knowledge of the super-essential? Through His unspeakable goodness, then, it pleased Him to be called by names that we could understand, that we might not be altogether cut off from the knowledge of Him but should have some notion of Him, however vague. Inasmuch, then, as He is incomprehensible, He is also unnameable. But inasmuch as He is the cause of all and contains in Himself the reasons and causes of all that is, He receives names drawn from all that is, even from opposites: for example, He is called light and darkness, water and fire: in order that we may know that these are not of His essence but that He is super-essential and unnameable: but inasmuch as He is the cause of all, He receives names from all His effects.

Wherefore, of the divine names, some have a negative signification, and indicate that He is super-essential : such are non-essential , timeless, without beginning, invisible: not that God is inferior to anything or lacking in anything (for all things are His and have become from Him and through Him and endure in Him Colossians 1:17), but that He is pre-eminently separated from all that is. For He is not one of the things that are, but over all things. Some again have an affirmative signification, as indicating that He is the cause of all things. For as the cause of all that is and of all essence, He is called both Ens and Essence. And as the cause of all reason and wisdom, of the rational and the wise, He is called both reason and rational, and wisdom and wise. Similarly He is spoken of as Intellect and Intellectual, Life and Living, Power and Powerful, and so on with all the rest. Or rather those names are most appropriate to Him which are derived from what is most precious and most akin to Himself. That which is immaterial is more precious and more akin to Himself than that which is material, and the pure than the impure, and the holy than the unholy: for they have greater part in Him. So then, sun and light will be more apt names for Him than darkness, and day than night, and life than death, and fire and spirit and water, as having life, than earth, and above all, goodness than wickedness: which is just to say, being more than not being. For goodness is existence and the cause of existence, but wickedness is the negation of goodness, that is, of existence. These, then, are the affirmations and the negations, but the sweetest names are a combination of both: for example, the super-essential essence, the Godhead that is more than God, the beginning that is above beginning and such like. Further there are some affirmations about God which have in a pre-eminent degree the force of denial: for example, darkness: for this does not imply that God is darkness but that He is not light, but above light.

God then is called Mind and Reason and Spirit and Wisdom and Power, as the cause of these, and as immaterial, and maker of all, and omnipotent. And these names are common to the whole Godhead, whether affirmative or negative. And they are also used of each of the subsistences of the Holy Trinity in the very same and identical way and with their full significance. For when I think of one of the subsistences, I recognise it to be perfect God and perfect essence: but when I combine and reckon the three together, I know one perfect God. For the Godhead is not compound but in three perfect subsistences, one perfect indivisible and uncompound God. And when I think of the relation of the three subsistences to each other, I perceive that the Father is super-essential Sun, source of goodness, fathomless sea of essence, reason, wisdom, power, light, divinity: the generating and productive source of good hidden in it. He Himself then is mind, the depth of reason, begetter of the Word, and through the Word the Producer of the revealing Spirit. And to put it shortly, the Father has no reason , wisdom, power, will , save the Son Who is the only power of the Father, the immediate cause of the creation of the universe: as perfect subsistence begotten of perfect subsistence in a manner known to Himself, Who is and is named the Son. And the Holy Spirit is the power of the Father revealing the hidden mysteries of His Divinity, proceeding from the Father through the Son in a manner known to Himself, but different from that of generation. Wherefore the Holy Spirit is the perfecter of the creation of the universe. All the terms, then, that are appropriate to the Father, as cause, source, begetter, are to be ascribed to the Father alone: while those that are appropriate to the caused, begotten Son, Word, immediate power, will, wisdom, are to be ascribed to the Son: and those that are appropriate to the caused, processional, manifesting, perfecting power, are to be ascribed to the Holy Spirit. The Father is the source and cause of the Son and the Holy Spirit: Father of the Son alone and producer of the Holy Spirit. The Son is Son, Word, Wisdom, Power, Image, Effulgence, Impress of the Father and derived from the Father. But the Holy Spirit is not the Son of the Father but the Spirit of the Father as proceeding from the Father. For there is no impulse without Spirit. And we speak also of the Spirit of the Son, not as through proceeding from Him, but as proceeding through Him from the Father. For the Father alone is cause.

Chapter 13. Concerning the place of God: and that the Deity alone is uncircumscribed.

Bodily place is the limit of that which contains, by which that which is contained is contained : for example, the air contains but the body is contained. But it is not the whole of the containing air which is the place of the contained body, but the limit of the containing air, where it comes into contact with the contained body: and the reason is clearly because that which contains is not within that which it contains.

But there is also mental place where mind is active, and mental and incorporeal nature exists: where mind dwells and energises and is contained not in a bodily but in a mental fashion. For it is without form, and so cannot be contained as a body is. God, then, being immaterial and uncircumscribed, has not place. For He is His own place, filling all things and being above all things, and Himself maintaining all things. Yet we speak of God having place and the place of God where His energy becomes manifest. For He penetrates everything without mixing with it, and imparts to all His energy in proportion to the fitness and receptive power of each: and by this I mean, a purity both natural and voluntary. For the immaterial is purer than the material, and that which is virtuous than that which is linked with vice. Wherefore by the place of God is meant that which has a greater share in His energy and grace. For this reason the Heaven is His throne. For in it are the angels who do His will and are always glorifying Him. For this is His rest and the earth is His footstool. Isaiah 66:1 For in it He dwelt in the flesh among men. Baruch 3:38 And His sacred flesh has been named the foot of God. The Church, too, is spoken of as the place of God: for we have set this apart for the glorifying of God as a sort of consecrated place wherein we also hold converse with Him. Likewise also the places in which His energy becomes manifest to us, whether through the flesh or apart from flesh, are spoken of as the places of God.

But it must be understood that the Deity is indivisible, being everywhere wholly in His entirety and not divided up part by part like that which has body, but wholly in everything and wholly above everything.

Marg. ms. Concerning the place of angel and spirit, and concerning the uncircumscribed.

The angel, although not contained in place with figured form as is body, yet is spoken of as being in place because he has a mental presence and energises in accordance with his nature, and is not elsewhere but has his mental limitations there where he energises. For it is impossible to energise at the same time in different places. For to God alone belongs the power of energising everywhere at the same time. The angel energises in different places by the quickness of his nature and the promptness and speed by which he can change his place: but the Deity, Who is everywhere and above all, energises at the same time in diverse ways with one simple energy.

Further the soul is bound up with the body. whole with whole and not part with part: and it is not contained by the body but contains it as fire does iron, and being in it energises with its own proper energies.

That which is comprehended in place or time or apprehension is circumscribed: while that which is contained by none of these is uncircumscribed. Wherefore the Deity alone is uncircumscribed, being without beginning and without end, and containing all things, and in no wise apprehended. For He alone is incomprehensible and unbounded, within no one's knowledge and contemplated by Himself alone. But the angel is circumscribed alike in time (for His being had commencement) and in place (but mental space, as we said above) and in apprehension. For they know somehow the nature of each other and have their bounds perfectly defined by the Creator. Bodies in short are circumscribed both in beginning and end, and bodily place and apprehension.

Marg. ms. From various sources concerning God and the Father, and the Son, and the Holy Spirit. And concerning the Word and the Spirit.

The Deity, then, is quite unchangeable and invariable. For all things which are not in our hands He has predetermined by His foreknowledge, each in its own proper and peculiar time and place. And accordingly *the Father judges no one, but has given all judgment to the Son.* John 5:22 For clearly the Father and the Son and also the Holy Spirit judged as God. But the Son Himself will descend in the body as man, and will sit on the throne of Glory (for descending and sitting require circumscribed body), and will judge all the world in justice.

All things are far apart from God, not in place but in nature. In our case, thoughtfulness, and wisdom, and counsel come to pass and go away as states of being. Not so in the case of God: for with Him there is no happening or ceasing to be: for He is invariable and unchangeable: and it would not be right to speak of contingency in connection with Him. For goodness is concomitant with essence. He who longs always after God, he sees Him: for God is in all things. Existing things are dependent on that which is, and nothing can be unless it is in that which is. God then is mingled with everything, maintaining their nature: and in His holy flesh the God-Word is made one in subsistence and is mixed with our nature, yet without confusion.

No one sees the Father, save the Son and the Spirit John 6:46 .

The Son is the counsel and wisdom and power of the Father. For one may not speak of quality in connection with God, from fear of implying that He was a compound of essence and quality.

The Son is from the Father, and derives from Him all His properties: *hence He cannot do ought of Himself.* For He has not energy peculiar to Himself and distinct from the Father.

That God Who is invisible by nature is made visible by His energies, we perceive from the organisation and government of the world Wisdom 12:5 .

The Son is the Father's image, and the Spirit the Son's, through which Christ dwelling in man makes him after his own image.

The Holy Spirit is God, being between the unbegotten and the begotten, and united to the Father through the Son. We speak of the Spirit of God, the Spirit of Christ, the mind of Christ, the Spirit of the Lord, the very Lord , the Spirit of adoption, of truth, of liberty, of wisdom (for He is the creator of all these): filling all things with essence, maintaining all things, filling the universe with essence, while yet the universe is not the measure of His power.

God is everlasting and unchangeable essence, creator of all that is, adored with pious consideration.

God is also Father, being ever unbegotten, for He was born of no one, but has begotten His co-eternal Son: God is likewise Son, being always with the

Father, born of the Father timelessly, everlastingly, without flux or passion, or separation from Him. God is also Holy Spirit, being sanctifying power, subsistential, proceeding from the Father without separation, and resting in the Son, identical in essence with Father and Son.

Word is that which is ever essentially present with the Father. Again, word is also the natural movement of the mind, according to which it is moved and thinks and considers, being as it were its own light and radiance. Again, word is the thought that is spoken only within the heart. And again, word is the utterance that is the messenger of thought. God therefore is Word essential and enhypostatic: and the other three kinds of word are faculties of the soul, and are not contemplated as having a proper subsistence of their own. The first of these is the natural offspring of the mind, ever welling up naturally out of it: the second is the thought: and the third is the utterance.

The Spirit has various meanings. There is the Holy Spirit: but the powers of the Holy Spirit are also spoken of as spirits: the good messenger is also spirit: the demon also is spirit: the soul too is spirit: and sometimes mind also is spoken of as spirit. Finally the wind is spirit and the air is spirit.

Chapter 14. The properties of the divine nature.

Uncreate, without beginning, immortal, infinite, eternal, immaterial , good, creative, just, enlightening, immutable, passionless, uncircumscribed, immeasurable, unlimited, undefined, unseen, unthinkable, wanting in nothing, being His own rule and authority, all-ruling, life-giving, omnipotent, of infinite power, containing and maintaining the universe and making provision for all: all these and such like attributes the Deity possesses by nature, not having received them from elsewhere, but Himself imparting all good to His own creations according to the capacity of each.

The subsistences dwell and are established firmly in one another. For they are inseparable and cannot part from one another, but keep to their separate courses within one another, without coalescing or mingling, but cleaving to each other. For the Son is in the Father and the Spirit: and the Spirit in the Father and the Son: and the Father in the Son and the Spirit, but there is no coalescence or commingling or confusion. And there is one and the same motion: for there is one impulse and one motion of the three subsistences, which is not to be observed in any created nature.

Further the divine effulgence and energy, being one and simple and indivisible, assuming many varied forms in its goodness among what is divisible and allotting to each the component parts of its own nature, still remains simple and is multiplied without division among the divided, and gathers and converts the divided into its own simplicity. For all things long after it and have their existence in it. It gives also to all things being according to their several natures , and it is itself the being of existing things, the life of living things, the reason of rational beings, the thought of thinking beings. But it is itself above mind and reason and life and essence.

Further the divine nature has the property of penetrating all things without mixing with them and of being itself impenetrable by anything else. Moreover, there is the property of knowing all things with a simple knowledge and of seeing all things, simply with His divine, all-surveying, immaterial eye, both the things of the present, and the things of the past, and the things of the future, before they come into being. Daniel 2:22 It is also sinless, and can cast sin out, and bring salvation: and all that it wills, it can accomplish, but does not will all it could accomplish. For it could destroy the universe but it does not will so to do.

BOOK II

Chapter 1. Concerning æon or age.

He created the ages Who Himself was before the ages, Whom the divine David thus addresses, *From age to age You are*. The divine apostle also says, *Through Whom He created the ages* Hebrews 1:2 .

It must then be understood that the word age has various meanings, for it denotes many things. The life of each man is called an age. Again, a period of a thousand years is called an age. Again, the whole course of the present life is called an age: also the future life, the immortal life after the resurrection , is spoken of as an age. Again, the word age is used to denote, not time nor yet a part of time as measured by the movement and course of the sun, that is to say, composed of days and nights, but the sort of temporal motion and interval that is co-extensive with eternity. For age is to things eternal just what time is to things temporal.

Seven ages of this world are spoken of, that is, from the creation of the heaven and earth till the general consummation and resurrection of men. For there is a partial consummation, viz., the death of each man: but there is also a general and complete consummation, when the general resurrection of men will come to pass. And the eighth age is the age to come.

Before the world was formed, when there was as yet no sun dividing day from night, there was not an age such as could be measured , but there was the sort of temporal motion and interval that is co-extensive with eternity. And in this sense there is but one age, and God is spoken of as αἰ&240·νιος and προαιώνιος, for the age or æon itself is His creation. For God, Who alone is without beginning, is Himself the Creator of all things, whether age or any other existing thing. And when I say God, it is evident that I mean the Father and His Only begotten Son, our Lord, Jesus Christ, and His all-holy Spirit, our one God.

But we speak also of ages of ages, inasmuch as the seven ages of the present world include many ages in the sense of lives of men, and the one age embraces all the ages, and the present and the future are spoken of as age of age. Further, everlasting (i.e. αἰ&240·νιος) life and everlasting punishment prove that the age or æon to come is unending. For time will not be counted by days and nights even after the resurrection, but there will rather be one day with no evening, wherein the Sun of Justice will shine brightly on the just, but for the sinful there will be night profound and limitless. In what way then will the period of one thousand years be counted which, according to Origen , is required for the complete restoration? Of all the ages, therefore, the sole creator is God Who has also created the universe and Who was before the ages.

Chapter 2. Concerning the creation.

Since, then, God, Who is good and more than good, did not find satisfaction in self-contemplation, but in His exceeding goodness wished certain things to come into existence which would enjoy His benefits and share in His goodness, He brought all things out of nothing into being and created them, both what is invisible and what is visible. Yea, even man, who is a compound of the visible and the invisible. And it is by thought that He creates, and thought is the basis of the work, the Word filling it and the Spirit perfecting it.

Chapter 3. Concerning angels.

He is Himself the Maker and Creator of the angels: for He brought them out of nothing into being and created them after His own image, an incorporeal race, a sort of spirit or immaterial fire: in the words of the divine David, *He makes His angels spirits, and His ministers a flame of fire* : and He has described their lightness and the ardour, and heat, and keenness and sharpness with which they hunger for God and serve Him, and how they are borne to the regions above and are quite delivered from all material thought.

An angel, then, is an intelligent essence, in perpetual motion, with free-will, incorporeal, ministering to God, having obtained by grace an immortal nature: and the Creator alone knows the form and limitation of its essence. But all that we can understand is, that it is incorporeal and immaterial. For all that is compared with God Who alone is incomparable, we find to be dense and material. For in reality only the Deity is immaterial and incorporeal.

The angel's nature then is rational, and intelligent, and endowed with free-will, changeable in will, or fickle. For all that is created is changeable, and only that which is un-created is unchangeable. Also all that is rational is endowed with free-will. As it is, then, rational and intelligent, it is endowed with free-will: and as it is created, it is changeable, having power either to abide or progress in goodness, or to turn towards evil.

It is not susceptible of repentance because it is incorporeal. For it is owing to the weakness of his body that man comes to have repentance.

It is immortal, not by nature but by grace. For all that has had beginning comes also to its natural end. But God alone is eternal, or rather, He is above the Eternal: for He, the Creator of times, is not under the dominion of time, but above time.

They are secondary intelligent lights derived from that first light which is without beginning, for they have the power of illumination; they have no need of tongue or hearing, but without uttering words they communicate to each other their own thoughts and counsels.

Through the Word, therefore, all the angels were created, and through the sanctification by the Holy Spirit were they brought to perfection, sharing each in proportion to his worth and rank in brightness and grace.

They are circumscribed: for when they are in the Heaven they are not on the earth: and when they are sent by God down to the earth they do not remain in the Heaven. They are not hemmed in by walls and doors, and bars and seals, for they are quite unlimited. Unlimited, I repeat, for it is not as they really are that they reveal themselves to the worthy men to whom God wishes them to appear, but in a changed form which the beholders are capable of seeing. For that alone is naturally and strictly unlimited which is un-created. For every created thing is limited by God Who created it.

Further, apart from their essence they receive the sanctification from the Spirit: through the divine grace they prophesy : they have no need of marriage for they are immortal.

Seeing that they are minds they are in mental places , and are not circumscribed after the fashion of a body. For they have not a bodily form by nature, nor are they extended in three dimensions. But to whatever post they may be assigned, there they are present after the manner of a mind and energise, and cannot be present and energise in various places at the same time.

Whether they are equals in essence or differ from one another we know not. God, their Creator, Who knows all things, alone knows. But they differ from each other in brightness and position, whether it is that their position is dependent on their brightness, or their brightness on their position: and they impart brightness to one another, because they excel one another in rank and nature. And clearly the higher share their brightness and knowledge with the lower.

They are mighty and prompt to fulfil the will of the Deity, and their nature is endowed with such celerity that wherever the Divine glance bids them there they are straightway found. They are the guardians of the divisions of the earth: they are set over nations and regions, allotted to them by their Creator: they govern all our affairs and bring us succour. And the reason surely is because they are set over us by the divine will and command and are ever in the vicinity of God.

With difficulty they are moved to evil, yet they are not absolutely immoveable: but now they are altogether immoveable, not by nature but by grace and by their nearness to the Only Good.

They behold God according to their capacity, and this is their food.

They are above us for they are incorporeal, and are free of all bodily passion, yet are not passionless: for the Deity alone is passionless.

They take different forms at the bidding of their Master, God, and thus reveal themselves to men and unveil the divine mysteries to them.

They have Heaven for their dwelling-place, and have one duty, to sing God's praise and carry out His divine will.

Moreover, as that most holy, and sacred, and gifted theologian, Dionysius the Areopagite , says, All theology, that is to say, the holy Scripture, has nine different names for the heavenly essences. These essences that divine master in sacred things divides into three groups, each containing three. And the first group, he says, consists of those who are in God's presence and are said to be directly and immediately one with Him, viz., the Seraphim with their six wings, the many-eyed Cherubim and those that sit in the holiest thrones. The second group is that of the Dominions, and the Powers, and the Authorities; and the third, and last, is that of the Rulers and Archangels and Angels.

Some, indeed , like Gregory the Theologian, say that these were before the creation of other things. He thinks that the angelic and heavenly powers were first and that thought was their function. Others, again, hold that they were created after the first heaven was made. But all are agreed that it was before the foundation of man. For myself, I am in harmony with the theologian. For it was fitting that the mental essence should be the first created, and then that which can be perceived, and finally man himself, in whose being both parts are united.

But those who say that the angels are creators of any kind of essence whatever are the mouth of their father, the devil. For since they are created things they are not creators. But He Who creates and provides for and maintains all things is God, Who alone is uncreate and is praised and glorified in the Father, the Son, and the Holy Spirit.

Chapter 4. Concerning the devil and demons.

He who from among these angelic powers was set over the earthly realm, and into whose hands God committed the guardianship of the earth, was not made wicked in nature but was good, and made for good ends, and received from his Creator no trace whatever of evil in himself. But he did not sustain the brightness and the honour which the Creator had bestowed on him, and of his free choice was changed from what was in harmony to what was at variance with his nature, and became roused against God Who created him, and determined to rise in rebellion against Him : and he was the first to depart from good and become evil. For evil is nothing else than absence of goodness, just as darkness also is absence of light. For goodness is the light of the mind, and, similarly, evil is the darkness of the mind. Light, therefore, being the work of the Creator and being made good (for *God saw all that He made, and behold they were exceeding good* Genesis 1:31) produced darkness at His free-will. But along with him an innumerable host of angels subject to him were torn away and followed him and shared in his fall. Wherefore, being of the same nature as the angels, they became wicked, turning away at their own free choice from good to evil.

Hence they have no power or strength against any one except what God in His dispensation has conceded to them, as for instance, against Job Job 1:12 and those swine that are mentioned in the Gospels. Mark 5:13 But when God has made the concession they do prevail, and are changed and transformed into any form whatever in which they wish to appear.

Of the future both the angels of God and the demons are alike ignorant: yet they make predictions. God reveals the future to the angels and commands them to prophesy, and so what they say comes to pass. But the demons also make predictions, sometimes because they see what is happening at a distance, and sometimes merely making guesses: hence much that they say is false and they should not be believed, even although they do often, in the way we have said, tell what is true. Besides they know the Scriptures.

All wickedness, then, and all impure passions are the work of their mind. But while the liberty to attack man has been granted to them, they have not the strength to over-master any one: for we have it in our power to receive or not to receive the attack. Wherefore there has been prepared for the devil and his demons, and those who follow him, fire unquenchable and everlasting punishment Matthew 25:41 .

Note, further, that what in the case of man is death is a fall in the case of angels. For after the fall there is no possibility of repentance for them, just as after death there is for men no repentance.

Chapter 5. Concerning the visible creation.

Our God Himself, Whom we glorify as Three in One, *created the heaven and the earth and all that they contain* , and brought all things out of nothing into being:

some He made out of no pre-existing basis of matter, such as heaven, earth, air, fire, water: and the rest out of these elements that He had created, such as living creatures, plants, seeds. For these are made up of earth, and water, and air, and fire, at the bidding of the Creator.

Chapter 6. Concerning the Heaven.

The heaven is the circumference of things created, both visible and invisible. For within its boundary are included and marked off both the mental faculties of the angels and all the world of sense. But the Deity alone is uncircumscribed, filling all things, and surrounding all things, and bounding all things, for He is above all things, and has created all things.

Since , therefore, the Scripture speaks of heaven, and heaven of heaven , and heavens of heavens , and the blessed Paul says that he was snatched away to the third heaven 2 Corinthians 12:2, we say that in the cosmogony of the universe we accept the creation of a heaven which the foreign philosophers, appropriating the views of Moses, call a starless sphere. But further, God called the firmament also heaven Genesis 1:8, which He commanded to be in the midst of the waters, setting it to divide the waters that are above the firmament from the waters that are below the firmament. And its nature, according to the divine Basilius , who is versed in the mysteries of divine Scripture, is delicate as smoke. Others, however, hold that it is watery in nature, since it is set in the midst of the waters: others say it is composed of the four elements: and lastly, others speak of it as a fifth body, distinct from the four elements.

Further, some have thought that the heaven encircles the universe and has the form of a sphere, and that everywhere it is the highest point, and that the centre of the space enclosed by it is the lowest part: and, further, that those bodies that are light and airy are allotted by the Creator the upper region: while those that are heavy and tend to descend occupy the lower region, which is the middle. The element, then, that is lightest and most inclined to soar upwards is fire, and hence they hold that its position is immediately after the heaven, and they call it ether, and after it comes the lower air. But earth and water, which are heavier and have more of a downward tendency, are suspended in the centre. Therefore, taking them in the reverse order, we have in the lowest situation earth and water: but water is lighter than earth, and hence is more easily set in motion: above these on all hands, like a covering, is the circle of air, and all round the air is the circle of ether, and outside air is the circle of the heaven.

Further, they say that the heaven moves in a circle and so compresses all that is within it, that they remain firm and not liable to fall asunder.

They say also that there are seven zones of the heaven , one higher than the other. And its nature, they say, is of extreme fineness, like that of smoke, and each zone contains one of the planets. For there are said to be seven planets: Sol, Luna, Jupiter, Mercury, Mars, Venus and Saturn. But sometimes Venus is called Lucifer and sometimes Vesper. These are called planets because their movements are the reverse of those of the heaven. For while the heaven and all other stars move from east to west, these alone move from west to east. And this can easily be seen in the case of the moon, which moves each evening a little backwards.

All, therefore, who hold that the heaven is in the form of a sphere, say that it is equally removed and distant from the earth at all points, whether above, or sideways, or below. And by 'below' and 'sideways' I mean all that comes within the range of our senses. For it follows from what has been said, that the heaven occupies the whole of the upper region and the earth the whole of the lower. They say, besides, that the heaven encircles the earth in the manner of a sphere, and bears along with it in its most rapid revolutions sun, moon and stars, and that when the sun is over the earth it becomes day there, and when it is under the earth it is night. And, again, when the sun goes under the earth it is night here, but day yonder.

Others have pictured the heaven as a hemisphere. This idea is suggested by these words of David, the singer of God, *Who stretches out the heavens like a curtain* , by which word he clearly means a tent: and by these from the blessed Isaiah, *Who has established the heavens like a vault* Isaiah 40:22: and also because when the sun, moon, and stars set they make a circuit round the earth from west to north, and so reach once more the east. Still, whether it is this way or that, all things have been made and established by the divine command, and have the divine will and counsel for a foundation that cannot be moved. *For He Himself spoke and they were made: He Himself commanded and they were created. He has also established them for ever and ever: He has made a decree which will not pass.*

The heaven of heaven, then, is the first heaven which is above the firmament. So here we have two heavens, for God called the firmament also Heaven. Genesis 1:8 And it is customary in the divine Scripture to speak of the air also as heavens, because we see it above us. *Bless Him*, it says, *all you birds of the heaven*, meaning of the air. For it is the air and not the heaven that is the region in which birds fly. So here we have three heavens, as the divine Apostle said. 2 Corinthians 12:2 But if you should wish to look upon the seven zones as seven heavens there is no injury done to the word of truth. For it is usual in the Hebrew tongue to speak of heaven in the plural, that is, as heavens, and when a Hebrew wishes to say heaven of heaven, he usually says heavens of heavens, and this clearly means heaven of heaven , which is above the firmament, and the waters which are above the heavens, whether it is the air and the firmament, or the seven zones of the firmament, or the firmament itself which are spoken of in the plural as heavens according to the Hebrew custom.

All things, then, which are brought into existence are subject to corruption according to the law of their nature , and so even the heavens themselves are corruptible. But by the grace of God they are maintained and preserved. Only the Deity, however, is by nature without beginning and without end. Wherefore it has been said, *They will perish, but You endure* : nevertheless, the heavens will not be utterly destroyed. For they will wax old and be wound round as a covering, and will be changed, and there will be a new heaven and a new earth Revelation 21:1 .

For the great part the heaven is greater than the earth, but we need not investigate the essence of the heaven, for it is quite beyond our knowledge.

It must not be supposed that the heavens or the luminaries are endowed with life. For they are inanimate and insensible. So that when the divine Scripture says, *Let the heavens rejoice and the earth be glad* , it is the angels in heaven and the men on earth that are invited to rejoice. For the Scripture is familiar with the figure of personification, and is wont to speak of inanimate things as though they were animate: for example , *The sea saw it and fled: Jordan was driven back.* And again, *What ailed you, O thou sea, that you fled, you, O Jordan, that you was driven back* ? Mountains, too, and hills are asked the reason of their leaping in the same way as we are wont to say, the city was gathered together, when we do not mean the buildings, but the inhabitants of the city: again, *the heavens declare the glory of God* , does not mean that they send forth a voice that can be heard by bodily ears, but that from their own greatness they bring before our minds the power of the Creator: and when we contemplate their beauty we praise the Maker as the Master-Craftsman.

Chapter 7. Concerning light, fire, the luminaries, sun, moon and stars.

Fire is one of the four elements, light and with a greater tendency to ascend than the others. It has the power of burning and also of giving light, and it was made by the Creator on the first day. For the divine Scripture says, *And God said, Let there be light, and there was light.* Genesis 1:3 Fire is not a different thing from what light is, as some maintain. Others again hold that this fire of the universe is above the air and call it ether. In the beginning, then, that is to say on the first day, God created light, the ornament and glory of the whole visible creation. For take away light and all things remain in undistinguishable darkness, incapable of displaying their native beauty. *And God called the light day, but the darkness He called night.* Genesis 1:5 Further, darkness is not any essence, but an accident: for it is simply absence of light. The air, indeed, has not light in its essence. It was, then, this very absence of light from the air that God called darkness: and it is not the essence of air that is darkness, but the absence of light which clearly is rather an accident than an essence. And, indeed, it was not night, but day, that was first named, so that day is first and after that comes night. Night, therefore, follows day. And from the beginning of day till the next day is one complete period of day and night. For the Scripture says, *And the evening and the morning were one day.*

When, therefore, in the first three days the light was poured forth and reduced at the divine command, both day and night came to pass. But on the fourth day God created the great luminary, that is, the sun, to have rule and authority over the day: for it is by it that day is made: for it is day when the sun is above the earth, and the duration of a day is the course of the sun over the earth from its rising till its setting. And He also created the lesser luminaries, that is, the moon and the stars, to have rule and authority over the night, and to give light by night. For it is night when the sun is under the earth, and the duration of night is the course of the sun under the earth from its rising till its setting. The moon, then, and the stars were set to lighten the night: not that they are in the daytime under the earth, for even by day stars are in the heaven over the earth but the sun conceals both the stars and the moon by the greater brilliance of its light and prevents them from being seen.

On these luminaries the Creator bestowed the first-created light: not because He was in need of other light, but that that light might not remain idle. For a luminary is not merely light, but a vessel for containing light.

There are, we are told, seven planets among these luminaries, and these move in a direction opposite to that of the heaven: hence the name planets. For, while they say that the heaven moves from east to west, the planets move from west to east; but the heaven bears the seven planets along with it by its swifter motion. Now these are the names of the seven planets: Luna, Mercury, Venus, Sol, Mars, Jupiter, Saturn, and in each zone of heaven is, we are told, one of these seven planets:

- In the first and highest Saturn

- In the second Jupiter

- In the third Mars

- In the fourth Sol

- In the fifth Venus

- In the sixth Mercury

- In the seventh and lowest Luna.

The course which the Creator appointed for them to run is unceasing and remains fixed as He established them. For the divine David says, *The moon and the stars which You established* , and by the word 'established,' he referred to the fixity and unchangeableness of the order and series granted to them by God. For He appointed them for seasons, and signs, and days and years. It is through the Sun that the four seasons are brought about. And the first of these is spring: for in it God created all things , and even down to the present time its presence is evidenced by the bursting of the flowers into bud, and this is the equinoctial period, since day and night each consist of twelve hours. It is caused by the sun rising in the middle, and is mild and increases the blood, and is warm and moist, and holds a position midway between winter and summer, being warmer and drier than winter, but colder and moister than summer. This season lasts from March 21st till June 24th. Next, when the rising of the sun moves towards more northerly parts, the season of summer succeeds, which has a place midway between spring and autumn, combining the warmth of spring with the dryness of autumn: for it is dry and warm, and increases the yellow bile. In it falls the longest day, which has fifteen hours, and the shortest night of all, having only nine hours. This season lasts from June 24th till September 25th. Then when the sun again returns to the middle, autumn takes the place of summer. It has a medium amount of cold and heat, dryness and moisture, and holds a place midway between summer and winter, combining the dryness of summer with the cold of winter. For it is cold and dry, and increases the black bile. This season, again, is equinoctial, both day and night consisting of twelve hours, and it lasts from September 25th till December 25th. And when the rising of the sun sinks to its smallest and lowest point, i.e. the south, winter is reached, with its cold and moisture. It occupies a place midway between autumn and spring, combining the cold of autumn and the moisture of spring. In it falls the shortest day, which has only nine hours, and the longest night, which has fifteen: and it lasts from December 25th till March 21st. For the Creator made this wise provision that we should not pass from the extreme of cold, or heat, or dryness, or moisture, to the opposite extreme, and thus incur grievous maladies. For reason itself teaches us the danger of sudden changes.

So, then, it is the sun that makes the seasons, and through them the year: it likewise makes the days and nights, the days when it rises and is above the earth, and the nights when it sets below the earth: and it bestows on the other luminaries, both moon and stars, their power of giving forth light.

Further, they say that there are in the heaven twelve signs made by the stars, and that these move in an opposite direction to the sun and moon, and the other five planets, and that the seven planets pass across these twelve signs.

Further, the sun makes a complete month in each sign and traverses the twelve signs in the same number of months. These, then, are the names of the twelve signs and their respective months:—

- The Ram, which receives the sun on the 21st of March.

- The Bull, on the 23rd of April.

- The Twins, on the 24th of May.

- The Crab, on the 24th of June.

- The Virgin, on the 25th of July.

- The Scales, on the 25th of September.

- The Scorpion, on the 25th of October.

- The Archer, on the 25th of November.

- Capricorn, on the 25th of December.

- Aquarius, on the 25th of January.

- The Fish, on the 24th of February.

But the moon traverses the twelve signs each month, since it occupies a lower position and travels through the signs at a quicker rate. For if you draw one circle within another, the inner one will be found to be the lesser: and so it is that owing to the moon occupying a lower position its course is shorter and is sooner completed.

Now the Greeks declare that all our affairs are controlled by the rising and setting and collision of these stars, viz., the sun and moon: for it is with these matters that astrology has to do. But we hold that we get from them signs of rain and drought, cold and heat, moisture and dryness, and of the various winds, and so forth , but no sign whatever as to our actions. For we have been created with free wills by our Creator and are masters over our own actions. Indeed, if all our actions depend on the courses of the stars, all we do is done of necessity : and necessity precludes either virtue or vice. But if we possess neither virtue nor vice, we do not deserve praise or punishment, and God, too, will turn out to be unjust, since He gives good things to some and afflicts others. Nay, He will no longer continue to guide or provide for His own creatures, if all things are carried and swept along in the grip of necessity. And the faculty of reason will be superfluous to us: for if we are not masters of any of our actions, deliberation is quite superfluous. Reason, indeed, is granted to us solely that we might take counsel, and hence all reason implies freedom of will.

And, therefore, we hold that the stars are not the causes of the things that occur, nor of the origin of things that come to pass, nor of the destruction of those things that perish. They are rather signs of showers and changes of air. But, perhaps, some one may say that though they are not the causes of wars, yet they are signs of them. And, in truth, the quality of the air which is produced by sun, and moon, and stars, produces in various ways different temperaments, and habits, and dispositions. But the habits are among the things that we have in our own hands, for it is reason that rules, and directs, and changes them.

It often happens, also, that comets arise. These are signs of the death of kings , and they are not any of the stars that were made in the beginning, but are formed at the same time by divine command and again dissolved. And so not even that star which the Magi saw at the birth of the Friend and Saviour of man, our Lord, Who became flesh for our sake, is of the number of those that were made in the beginning. And this is evidently the case because sometimes its course was from east to west, and sometimes from north to south; at one moment it was hidden, and at the next it was revealed: which is quite out of harmony with the order and nature of the stars.

It must be understood, then, that the moon derives its light from the sun; not that God was unable to grant it light of its own, but in order that rhythm and order may be unimpressed upon nature, one part ruling, the other being ruled, and that we might thus be taught to live in community and to share our possessions with one another, and to be under subjection, first to our Maker and Creator, our God and Master, and then also to the rulers set in authority over us by Him: and not to question why this man is ruler and not I myself, but to welcome all that comes from God in a gracious and reasonable spirit.

The sun and the moon, moreover, suffer eclipse, and this demonstrates the folly of those who worship the creature in place of the Creator Romans 1:25, and teaches us how changeable and alterable all things are. For all things are changeable save God, and whatever is changeable is liable to corruption in accordance with the laws of its own nature.

Now the cause of the eclipse of the sun is that the body of the moon is interposed like a partition-wall and casts a shadow, and prevents the light from being shed down on us : and the extent of the eclipse is proportional to the size of the moon's body that is found to conceal the sun. But do not marvel that the moon's body is the smaller. For many declare that the sun is many times larger even than the earth, and the holy Fathers say that it is equal to the earth: yet often a small cloud, or even a small hill or a wall quite conceals it.

The eclipse of the moon, on the other hand, is due to the shadow the earth casts on it when it is a fifteen days' moon and the sun and moon happen to be at the opposite poles of the highest circle, the sun being under the earth and the moon above the earth. For the earth casts a shadow and the sun's light is prevented from illuminating the moon, and therefore it is then eclipsed.

It should be understood that the moon was made full by the Creator, that is, a fifteen days' moon: for it was fitting that it should be made complete. But on the fourth day, as we said, the sun was created. Therefore the moon was eleven days in advance of the sun, because from the fourth to the fifteenth day there are eleven days. Hence it happens that in each year the twelve months of the moon contain eleven days fewer than the twelve months of the sun. For the twelve months of the sun contain three hundred and sixty-five and a quarter days, and so because the quarter becomes a whole, in four years an extra day is completed, which is called bis-sextile. And that year has three hundred and sixty-six days. The years of the moon, on the other hand, have three hundred and fifty-four days. For the moon wanes from the time of its origin, or renewal, till it is fourteen and three-quarter days' old, and proceeds to wane till the twenty-ninth and a half day, when it is completely void of light. And then when it is once more connected with the sun it is reproduced and renewed, a memorial of our resurrection. Thus in each year the moon gives away eleven days to the sun, and so in three years the intercalary month of the Hebrews arises, and that year comes to consist of thirteen months, owing to the addition of these eleven days.

It is evident that both sun and moon and stars are compound and liable to corruption according to the laws of their various natures. But of their nature we are ignorant. Some, indeed, say that fire when deprived of matter is invisible, and thus, that when it is quenched it vanishes altogether. Others, again, say that when it is quenched it is transformed into air.

The circle of the zodiac has an oblique motion and is divided into twelve sections called zodia, or signs: each sign has three divisions of ten each, i.e. thirty divisions, and each division has sixty very minute subdivisions. The heaven, therefore, has three hundred and sixty-five degrees: the hemisphere above the earth and that below the earth each having one hundred and eighty degrees.

The abodes of the planets.

The Ram and the Scorpion are the abode of Mars: the Bull and the Scales, of Venus : the Twins and the Virgin, of Mercury: the Crab, of the Moon: the Lion, of the Sun: the Archer and the Fish, of Jupiter: Capricorn and Aquarius, of Saturn.

Their altitudes.

The Ram has the altitude of the Sun: the Bull, of the Moon: the Crab, of Jupiter: the Virgin, of Mars: the Scales, of Saturn: Capricorn, of Mercury: the Fish, of Venus.

The phases of the moon.

It is in conjunction whenever it is in the same degree as the sun: it is born when it is fifteen degrees distant from the sun: it rises when it is crescent-shaped, and this occurs twice , at which times it is sixty degrees distant from the sun: it is half-full twice, when it is ninety degrees from the sun: twice it is gibbous, when it is one hundred and twenty degrees from the sun: it is twice a full moon, giving full light, when it is a hundred and fifty degrees from the sun: it is a complete moon when it is a hundred and eighty degrees distant from the sun. We say twice, because these phases occur both when the moon waxes and when it wanes. In two and a half days the moon traverses each sign.

Chapter 8. Concerning air and winds.

Air is the most subtle element, and is moist and warm: heavier, indeed, than fire: but lighter than earth and water: it is the cause of respiration and voice: it is colorless, that is, it has no color by nature: it is clear and transparent, for it is capable of receiving light: it ministers to three of our senses, for it is by its aid that we see, hear and smell: it has the power likewise of receiving heat and cold, dryness and moisture, and its movements in space are up, down, within, without, to the right and to the left, and the cyclical movement.

It does not derive its light from itself, but is illuminated by sun, and moon, and stars, and fire. And this is just what the Scripture means when it says, *And darkness was upon the deep* Genesis 1:2; for its object is to show that the air has not derived its light from itself, but that it is quite a different essence from light.

And wind is a movement of air: or wind is a rush of air which changes its name as it changes the place whence it rushes.

Its place is in the air. For place is the circumference of a body. But what is it that surrounds bodies but air? There are, moreover, different places in which the movement of air originates, and from these the winds get their names. There are in all twelve winds. It is said that air is just fire after it has been extinguished, or the vapour of heated water. At all events, in its own special nature the air is warm, but it becomes cold owing to the proximity of water and earth, so that the lower parts of it are cold, and the higher warm.

These then are the winds : Cæcias, or Meses, arises in the region where the sun rises in summer. Subsolanus, where the sun rises at the equinoxes. Eurus, where it rises in winter. Africus, where it sets in winter. Favonius, where it sets at the equinoxes, and Corus, or Olympias, or Iapyx, where it sets in summer. Then come Auster and Aquilo, whose blasts oppose one another. Between Aquilo and Cæcias comes Boreas: and between Eurus and Auster, Phœnix or Euronotus; between Auster and Africus, Libonotus or Leuconotus: and lastly, between Aquilo and Corus, Thrascias, or Cercius, as it is called by the inhabitants of that region.

[These , then, are the races which dwell at the ends of the world: beside Subsolanus are the Bactriani: beside Eurus, the Indians: beside Phœnix, the Red Sea and Ethiopia: beside Libonotus, the Garamantes, who are beyond Systis: beside Africus, the Ethiopians and the Western Mauri: beside Favonius, the columns of Hercules and the beginnings of Libya and Europe: beside Corus, Iberia, which is now called Spain: beside Thrascia, the Gauls and the neighbouring nations: beside Aquilo, the Scythians who are beyond Thrace: beside Boreas, Pontus, Mæotis and the Sarmatæ: beside Cæcias, the Caspian Sea and the Sacai.]

Chapter 9. Concerning the waters.

Water also is one of the four elements, the most beautiful of God's creations. It is both wet and cold, heavy, and with a tendency to descend, and flows with great readiness. It is this the Holy Scripture has in view when it says, *And darkness was upon the face of the deep. And the Spirit of God moved upon the face of the waters.* Genesis 1:2 For the deep is nothing else than a huge quantity of water whose limit man cannot comprehend. In the beginning, indeed, the water lay all over the surface of the earth. And first God created the firmament to divide the water above the firmament from the water below the firmament. For in the midst of the sea of waters the firmament was established at the Master's decree. And out of it God bade the firmament arise, and it arose. Now for what reason was it that God placed water above the firmament? It was because of the intense burning heat of the sun and ether. For immediately under the firmament is spread out the ether , and the sun and moon and stars are in the firmament, and so if water had not been put above it the firmament would have been consumed by the heat.

Next, God bade the waters be gathered together into one mass. Genesis 1:9 But when the Scripture speaks of one mass it evidently does not mean that they were gathered together into one place: for immediately it goes on to say, *And the gatherings of the waters He called seas* Genesis 1:10: but the words signify that the waters were separated off in a body from the earth into distinct groups. Thus the waters were gathered together into their special collections and the dry land was brought to view. And hence arose the two seas that surround Egypt, for it lies between two seas. These collections contain various seas and mountains, and islands, and promontories, and harbours, and surround various bays and beaches, and coastlands. For the word beach is used when the nature of the tract is sandy, while coastland signifies that it is rocky and deep close into shore, getting deep all on a sudden. In like manner arose also the sea that lies where the sun rises, the name of which is the Indian Sea: also the northern sea called the Caspian. The lakes also were formed in the same manner.

The ocean, then, is like a river encircling the whole earth, and I think it is concerning it that the divine Scripture says, *A river went out of Paradise.* Genesis 2:10 The water of the ocean is sweet and potable. It is it that furnishes the seas with water which, because it stays a long time in the seas and stands unmoved, becomes bitter: for the sun and the waterspouts draw up always the finer parts. Thus it is that clouds are formed and showers take place, because the filtration makes the water sweet.

This is parted into four first divisions, that is to say, into four rivers. The name of the first is Pheison, which is the Indian Ganges; the name of the second is Geon, which is the Nile flowing from Ethiopia down to Egypt: the name of the third is Tigris, and the name of the fourth is Euphrates. There are also very many other mighty rivers of which some empty themselves into the sea and others are used up in the earth. Thus the whole earth is bored through and mined, and has, so to speak, certain veins through which it sends up in springs the water it has received from the sea. The water of the spring thus depends for its character on the quality of the earth. For the sea water is filtered and strained through the earth and thus becomes sweet. But if the place from which the spring arises is bitter or briny, so also is the water that is sent up. Moreover, it often happens that water which has been closely pent up bursts through with violence, and thus it becomes warm. And this is why they send forth waters that are naturally warm.

By the divine decree hollow places are made in the earth, and so into these the waters are gathered. And this is how mountains are formed. God, then, bade the first water produce living breath, since it was to be by water and the Holy Spirit that moved upon the waters in the beginning Genesis 1:2, that man was to be renewed. For this is what the divine Basilius said: Therefore it produced living creatures, small and big; whales and dragons, fish that swim in the waters, and feathered fowl. The birds form a link between water and earth and air: for they have their origin in the water, they live on the earth and they fly in the air. Water, then, is the most beautiful element and rich in usefulness, and purifies from all filth, and not only from the filth of the body but from that of the soul, if it should have received the grace of the Spirit.

Concerning the seas.

The Ægean Sea is received by the Hellespont, which ends at Abydos and Sestus: next, the Propontis, which ends at Chalcedon and Byzantium: here are the straits where the Pontus arises. Next, the lake of Mæotis. Again, from the beginning of Europe and Libya it is the Iberian Sea, which extends from the pillars of Hercules to the Pyrenees mountain. Then the Ligurian Sea as far as the borders of Etruria. Next, the Sardinian Sea, which is above Sardinia and inclines downwards to Libya. Then the Etrurian Sea, which begins at the extreme limits of Liguria and ends at Sicily. Then the Libyan Sea. Then the Cretan, and Sicilian, and Ionian, and Adriatic Seas, the last of which is poured out of the Sicilian Sea, which is called the Corinthian Gulf, or the Alcyonian Sea. The Saronic Sea is surrounded by the Sunian and Scyllæan Seas. Next is the Myrtoan Sea and the Icarian Sea, in which are also the Cyclades. Then the Carpathian, and Pamphylian, and Egyptian Seas: and, thereafter, above the Icarian Sea, the Ægean Sea pours itself out. There is also the coast of Europe from the mouth of the Tanais River to the Pillars of Hercules, 609,709 stadia: and that of Libya from the Tigris, as far as the mouth of the Canobus, 209,252 stadia: and lastly, that of Asia from the Canobus to the Tanais, which, including the Gulf, is 4,111 stadia. And so the full extent of the seaboard of the world that we inhabit with the gulfs is 1,309,072 stadia.

Chapter 10. Concerning earth and its products.

The earth is one of the four elements, dry, cold, heavy, motionless, brought into being by God, out of nothing on the first day. *For in the beginning*, he said, *God created the heaven and the earth* Genesis 1:1: but the seat and foundation of the earth no man has been able to declare. Some, indeed, hold that its seat is the waters: thus the divine David says, *To Him Who established the earth on the waters*. Others place it in the air. Again some other says, *He Who hangs the earth on nothing.* Job 26:7 And, again, David, the singer of God, says, as though the representative of God, *I bear up the pillars of it* , meaning by pillars the force that sustains it. Further, the expression, *He has founded it upon the seas* , shows clearly that the earth is on all hands surrounded with water. But whether we grant that it is established on itself, or on air or on water, or on nothing, we must not turn aside from reverent thought, but must admit that all things are sustained and preserved by the power of the Creator.

In the beginning, then, as the Holy Scripture says Genesis 1:2, it was hidden beneath the waters, and was unwrought, that is to say, not beautified. But at God's bidding, places to hold the waters appeared, and then the mountains came into existence, and at the divine command the earth received its own proper adornment, and was dressed in all manner of herbs and plants, and on these, by the divine decree, was bestowed the power of growth and nourishment, and of producing seed to generate their like. Moreover, at the bidding of the Creator it produced also all manner of kinds of living creatures, creeping things, and wild beasts, and cattle. All, indeed, are for the seasonable use of man: but of them some are for food, such as stags, sheep, deer, and such like: others for service such as camels, oxen, horses, asses, and such like: and others for enjoyment, such as apes, and among birds, jays and parrots, and such like. Again, among plants and herbs some are fruit bearing, others edible, others fragrant and flowery, given to us for our enjoyment, for example, the rose and such like, and others for the healing of disease. For there is not a single animal or plant in which the Creator has not implanted some form of energy capable of being used to satisfy man's needs. For He Who knew all things before they were, saw that in the future man would go forward in the strength of his own will, and would be subject to corruption, and, therefore, He created all things for his seasonable use, alike those in the firmament, and those on the earth, and those in the waters.

Indeed, before the transgression all things were under his power. For God set him as ruler over all things on the earth and in the waters. Even the serpent was accustomed to man, and approached him more readily than it did other living creatures, and held intercourse with him with delightful motions. And hence it was through it that the devil, the prince of evil, made his most wicked suggestion to our first parents. Genesis 3:1 Moreover, the earth of its own accord used to yield fruits, for the benefit of the animals that were obedient to man, and there was neither rain nor tempest on the earth. But after the transgression, when he was compared with the unintelligent cattle and became like to them , after he had contrived that in him irrational desire should have rule over reasoning mind and had become disobedient to the Master's command, the subject creation rose up against him whom the Creator had appointed to be ruler: and it was appointed for him that he should till with sweat the earth from which he had been taken.

But even now wild beasts are not without their uses, for, by the terror they cause, they bring man to the knowledge of his Creator and lead him to call upon His name. And, further, at the transgression the thorn sprung out of the earth in accordance with the Lord's express declaration and was conjoined with the pleasures of the rose, that it might lead us to remember the transgression on account of which the earth was condemned to bring forth for us thorns and prickles.

That this is the case is made worthy of belief from the fact that their endurance is secured by the word of the Lord, saying, *Be fruitful and multiply, and replenish the earth* Genesis 1:22 .

Further, some hold that the earth is in the form of a sphere, others that it is in that of a cone. At all events it is much smaller than the heaven, and suspended almost like a point in its midst. And it will pass away and be changed. But blessed is the man who inherits the earth promised to the meek Matthew 5:5 .

For the earth that is to be the possession of the holy is immortal. Who, then, can fitly marvel at the boundless and incomprehensible wisdom of the Creator? Or who can render sufficient thanks to the Giver of so many blessings ?

[There are also provinces, or prefectures, of the earth which we recognise: Europe embraces thirty four, and the huge continent of Asia has forty-eight of these provinces, and twelve canons as they are called.]

Chapter 11. Concerning Paradise.

Now when God was about to fashion man out of the visible and invisible creation in His own image and likeness to reign as king and ruler over all the earth and all that it contains, He first made for him, so to speak, a kingdom in which he should live a life of happiness and prosperity. And this is the divine paradise , planted in Eden by the hands of God, a very storehouse of joy and gladness of heart (for Eden means luxuriousness). Its site is higher in the East than all the earth: it is temperate and the air that surrounds it is the rarest and purest: evergreen plants are its pride, sweet fragrances abound, it is flooded with light, and in sensuous freshness and beauty it transcends imagination: in truth the place is divine, a meet home for him who was created in God's image: no creature lacking reason made its dwelling there but man alone, the work of God's own hands.

In its midst God planted the tree of life and the tree of knowledge. Genesis 2:9 The tree of knowledge was for trial, and proof, and exercise of man's obedience and disobedience: and hence it was named the tree of the knowledge of good and evil, or else it was because to those who partook of it was given power to know their own nature. Now this is a good thing for those who are mature, but an evil thing for the immature and those whose appetites are too strong , being like solid food to tender babes still in need of milk. For our Creator, God, did not intend us to be burdened with care and troubled about many things, nor to take thought about, or make provision for, our own life. But this at length was Adam's fate: for he tasted and knew that he was naked and made a girdle round about him: for he took fig-leaves and girded himself about. But before they took of the fruit, *They were both naked, Adam and Eve, and were not ashamed.* Genesis 2:25 For God meant that we should be thus free from passion, and this is indeed the mark of a mind absolutely void of passion. Yea, He meant us further to be free from care and to have but one work to perform, to sing as do the angels, without ceasing or intermission, the praises of the Creator, and to delight in contemplation of Him and to cast all our care on Him. This is what the Prophet David proclaimed to us when He said, *Cast your burden on the Lord, and He will sustain you.* And, again, in the Gospels, Christ taught His disciples saying, *Take no thought for your life what you shall eat, nor for your body what you shall put on.* Matthew 6:25 And further, *Seek ye first the Kingdom of God and His righteousness and all these things shall be added unto you.* And to Martha He said, *Martha, Martha, you are careful and troubled about many things: but one thing is needful: and Mary has chosen that good part, which shall not be taken away from her* Luke 10:41-42, meaning, clearly, sitting at His feet and listening to His words.

The tree of life, on the other hand, was a tree having the energy that is the cause of life, or to be eaten only by those who deserve to live and are not subject to death. Some, indeed, have pictured Paradise as a realm of sense , and others as a realm of mind. But it seems to me, that, just as man is a creature, in whom we find both sense and mind blended together, in like manner also man's most holy temple combines the properties of sense and mind, and has this twofold expression: for, as we said, the life in the body is spent in the most divine and lovely region, while the life in the soul is passed in a place far more sublime and of more surpassing beauty, where God makes His home, and where He wraps man about as with a glorious garment, and robes him in His grace, and delights and sustains him like an angel with the sweetest of all fruits, the contemplation of Himself. Verily it has been fitly named the tree of life. For since the life is not cut short by death, the sweetness of the divine participation is imparted to those who share it. And this is, in truth, what God meant by every tree, saying, *Of every tree in Paradise you may freely eat.* Genesis 2:16 For the 'every' is just Himself in Whom and through Whom the universe is maintained. But the tree of the knowledge of good and evil was for the distinguishing between the many divisions of contemplation, and this is just the knowledge of one's own nature, which, indeed, is a good thing for those who are mature and advanced in divine contemplation (being of itself a proclamation of the magnificence of God), and have no fear of falling , because they have through time come to have the habit of such contemplation, but it is an evil thing to those still young and with stronger appetites, who by reason of their insecure hold on the better part, and because as yet they are not firmly established in the seat of the one and only good, are apt to be torn and dragged away from this to the care of their own body.

Thus, to my thinking, the divine Paradise is twofold, and the God-inspired Fathers handed down a true message, whether they taught this doctrine or that. Indeed, it is possible to understand by every tree the knowledge of the divine power derived from created things. In the words of the divine Apostle, *For the invisible things of Him from the creation of the world are clearly seen, being understood by the things that are made.* Romans 1:20 But of all these thoughts and speculations the sublimest is that dealing with ourselves, that is, with our own composition. As the divine David says, *The knowledge of You from me* , that is from my constitution, was made a wonder. But for the reasons we have already mentioned, such knowledge was dangerous for Adam who had been so lately created.

The tree of life too may be understood as that more divine thought that has its origin in the world of sense, and the ascent through that to the originating and constructive cause of all. And this was the name He gave to every tree, implying fullness and indivisibility, and conveying only participation in what is good. But by the tree of the knowledge of good and evil, we are to understand that sensible and pleasurable food which, sweet though it seems, in reality brings him who partakes of it into communion with evil. For God says, *Of every tree in Paradise you may freely eat.* Genesis 2:16 It is, me-thinks, as if God said, *Through all My creations you are to ascend to Me your creator, and of all the fruits you may pluck one, that is, Myself who art the true life: let every thing bear for you the fruit of life, and let participation in Me be the support of your own being. For in this way you will be immortal. But of the tree of the knowledge of good and evil, you shall not eat of it: for in the day that you eat thereof you shall surely die.* For sensible food is by nature for the replenishing of that which gradually wastes away and it passes into the drought and perishes: and he cannot remain incorruptible who partakes of sensible food.

Chapter 12. Concerning Man.

In this way, then, God brought into existence mental essence , by which I mean, angels and all the heavenly orders. For these clearly have a mental and incorporeal nature: incorporeal I mean in comparison with the denseness of matter. For the Deity alone in reality is immaterial and incorporeal. But further He created in the same way sensible essence , that is heaven and earth and the intermediate region; and so He created both the kind of being that is of His own nature (for the nature that has to do with reason is related to God, and apprehensible by mind alone), and the kind which, inasmuch as it clearly falls under the province of the senses, is separated from Him by the greatest interval. And it was also fit that there should be a mixture of both kinds of being, as a token of still greater wisdom and of the opulence of the Divine expenditure as regards natures, as Gregorius, the expounder of God's being and ways, puts it, and to be a sort of connecting link between the visible and invisible natures. And by the word fit I mean, simply that it was an evidence of the Creator's will, for that will is the law and ordinance most meet, and no one will say to his Maker, Why have You so fashioned me? For the potter is able at his will to make vessels of various patterns out of his clay Romans 9:21, as a proof of his own wisdom.

Now this being the case, He creates with His own hands man of a visible nature and an invisible, after His own image and likeness: on the one hand man's body He formed of earth, and on the other his reasoning and thinking soul He bestowed upon him by His own inbreathing, and this is what we mean by after His image. For the phrase after His image clearly refers to the side of his nature which consists of mind and free will, whereas after His likeness means likeness in virtue so far as that is possible.

Further, body and soul were formed at one and the same time , not first the one and then the other, as Origen so senselessly supposes.

God then made man without evil, upright, virtuous, free from pain and care, glorified with every virtue, adorned with all that is good, like a sort of second microcosm within the great world , another angel capable of worship, compound, surveying the visible creation and initiated into the mysteries of the realm of thought, king over the things of earth, but subject to a higher king, of the earth and of the heaven, temporal and eternal, belonging to the realm of sight and to the realm of thought, midway between greatness and lowliness, spirit and flesh: for he is spirit by grace, but flesh by overweening pride: spirit that he may abide and glorify his Benefactor, and flesh that he may suffer, and suffering may be admonished and disciplined when he prides himself in his greatness : here, that is, in the present life, his life is ordered as an animal's, but elsewhere, that is, in the age to come, he is changed and — to complete the mystery— becomes deified by merely inclining himself towards God; becoming deified, in the way of participating in the divine glory and not in that of a change into the divine being.

But God made him by nature sinless, and endowed him with free will. By sinless, I mean not that sin could find no place in him (for that is the case with Deity alone), but that sin is the result of the free volition he enjoys rather than an integral part of his nature ; that is to say, he has the power to continue and go forward in the path of goodness, by co-operating with the divine grace, and likewise to turn from good and take to wickedness, for God has conceded this by conferring freedom of will upon him. For there is no virtue in what is the result of mere force.

The soul, accordingly , is a living essence, simple, incorporeal, invisible in its proper nature to bodily eyes, immortal, reasoning and intelligent, formless, making use of an organised body, and being the source of its powers of life, and growth, and sensation, and generation , mind being but its purest part and not in any wise alien to it; (for as the eye to the body, so is the mind to the soul); further it enjoys freedom and volition and energy, and is mutable, that is, it is given to change, because it is created. All these qualities according to nature it has received of the grace of the Creator, of which grace it has received both its being and this particular kind of nature.

Marg. The different applications of incorporeal. We understand two kinds of what is incorporeal and invisible and formless: the one is such in essence, the other by free gift: and likewise the one is such in nature, and the other only in comparison with the denseness of matter. God then is incorporeal by nature, but the angels and demons and souls are said to be so by free gift, and in comparison with the denseness of matter.

Further, body is that which has three dimensions, that is to say, it has length and breadth and depth, or thickness. And every body is composed of the four elements; the bodies of living creatures, moreover, are composed of the four humours.

Now there are, it should be known, four elements: earth which is dry and cold: water which is cold and wet: air which is wet and warm: fire which is warm and dry. In like manner there are also four humours, analogous to the four elements: black bile, which bears an analogy to earth, for it is dry and cold: phlegm, analogous to water, for it is cold and wet: blood, analogous to air , for it is wet and warm: yellow bile, the analogue to fire, for it is warm and dry. Now, fruits are composed of the elements, and the humours are composed of the fruits, and the bodies of living creatures consist of the humours and dissolve back into them. For every thing that is compound dissolves back into its elements.

Marg. That man has community alike with inanimate things and animate creatures, whe ther they are devoid of or possess the faculty of reason.

Man, it is to be noted, has community with things inanimate, and participates in the life of unreasoning creatures, and shares in the mental processes of those endowed with reason. For the bond of union between man and inanimate things is the body and its composition out of the four elements: and the bond between man and plants consists, in addition to these things, of their powers of nourishment and growth and seeding, that is, generation: and finally, over and above these links man is connected with unreasoning animals by appetite, that is anger and desire, and sense and impulsive movement.

There are then five senses, sight, hearing, smell, taste, touch. Further, impulsive movement consists in change from place to place, and in the movements of the body as a whole and in the emission of voice and the drawing of breath. For we have it in our power to perform or refrain from performing these actions.

Lastly, man's reason unites him to incorporeal and intelligent natures, for he applies his reason and mind and judgment to everything, and pursues after virtues, and eagerly follows after piety, which is the crown of the virtues. And so man is a microcosm.

Moreover, it should be known that division and flux and change are peculiar to the body alone. By change, I mean change in quality, that is in heat and cold and so forth: by flux, I mean change in the way of depletion , for dry things and wet things and spirit suffer depletion, and require repletion: so that hunger and thirst are natural affections. Again, division is the separation of the humours, one from another, and the partition into form and matter.

But piety and thought are the peculiar properties of the soul. And the virtues are common to soul and body, although they are referred to the soul as if the soul were making use of the body.

The reasoning part, it should be understood, naturally bears rule over that which is void of reason. For the faculties of the soul are divided into that which has reason, and that which is without reason. Again, of that which is without reason there are two divisions: that which does not listen to reason, that is to say, is disobedient to reason, and that which listens and obeys reason. That which does not listen or obey reason is the vital or pulsating faculty, and the spermatic or generative faculty, and the vegetative or nutritive faculty: to this belong also the faculties of growth and bodily formation. For these are not under the dominion of reason but under that of nature. That which listens to and obeys reason, on the other hand is divided into anger and desire. And the unreasoning part of the soul is called in common the pathetic and the appetitive. Further, it is to be understood, that impulsive movement likewise belongs to the part that is obedient to reason.

The part which does not pay heed to reason includes the nutritive and generative and pulsating faculties: and the name vegetative is applied to the faculties of increase and nutriment and generation, and the name vital to the faculty of pulsation.

Of the faculty of nutrition, then, there are four forces: an attractive force which attracts nourishment: a retentive force by which nourishment is retained and not suffered to be immediately excreted: an alternative force by which the food is resolved into the humours: and an excretive force, by which the excess of food is excreted into the draught and cast forth.

The forces again , inherent in a living creature are, it should be noted, partly psychical, partly vegetative, partly vital. The psychical forces are concerned with free volition, that is to say, impulsive movement and sensation. Impulsive movement includes change of place and movement of the body as a whole, and phonation and respiration. For it is in our power to perform or refrain from performing these acts. The vegetative and vital forces, however, are quite outside the province of will. The vegetative, moreover, include the faculties of nourishment and growth, and generation, and the vital power is the faculty of pulsation. For these go on energising whether we will it or not.

Lastly, we must observe that of actual things, some are good, and some are bad. A good thing in anticipation constitutes desire: while a good thing in realisation constitutes pleasure. Similarly an evil thing in anticipation begets fear, and in realisation it begets pain. And when we speak of good in this connection we are to be understood to mean both real and apparent good: and, similarly, we mean real and apparent evil.

Chapter 13. Concerning Pleasures.

There are pleasures of the soul and pleasures of the body. The pleasures of the soul are those which are the exclusive possession of the soul, such as the pleasures of learning and contemplation. The pleasures of the body, however, are those which are enjoyed by soul and body in fellowship, and hence are called bodily pleasures: and such are the pleasures of food and intercourse and the like. But one could not find any class of pleasures belonging solely to the body.

Again, some pleasures are true, others false. And the exclusively intellectual pleasures consist in knowledge and contemplation, while the pleasures of the body depend upon sensation. Further, of bodily pleasures , some are both natural and necessary, in the absence of which life is impossible, for example the pleasures of food which replenishes waste, and the pleasures of necessary clothing. Others are natural but not necessary, as the pleasures of natural and lawful intercourse. For though the function that these perform is to secure the permanence of the race as a whole, it is still possible to live a virgin life apart from them. Others, however, are neither natural nor necessary, such as drunkenness, lust, and surfeiting to excess. For these contribute neither to the maintenance of our own lives nor to the succession of the race, but on the contrary, are rather even a hindrance. He therefore that would live a life acceptable to God must follow after those pleasures which are both natural and necessary: and must give a secondary place to those which are natural but not necessary, and enjoy them only in fitting season, and manner, and measure; while the others must be altogether renounced.

Those then are to be considered moral pleasures which are not bound up with pain, and bring no cause for repentance, and result in no other harm and keep within the bounds of moderation, and do not draw us far away from serious occupations, nor make slaves of us.

Chapter 14. Concerning Pain.

There are four varieties of pain, viz., anguish , grief , envy, pity. Anguish is pain without utterance: grief is pain that is heavy to bear like a burden: envy is pain over the good fortune of others: pity is pain over the evil fortune of others.

Chapter 15. Concerning Fear.

Fear is divided into six varieties: viz., shrinking , shame, disgrace, consternation, panic, anxiety. Shrinking is fear of some act about to take place. Shame is fear arising from the anticipation of blame: and this is the highest form of the affection. Disgrace is fear springing from some base act already done, and even for this form there is some hope of salvation. Consternation is fear originating in some huge product of the imagination. Panic is fear caused by some unusual product of the imagination. Anxiety is fear of failure, that is, of misfortune: for when we fear that our efforts will not meet with success, we suffer anxiety.

Chapter 16. Concerning Anger.

Anger is the ebullition of the heart's blood produced by bilious exhalation or turbidity. Hence it is that the words χολή and χόλος are both used in the sense of anger. Anger is sometimes lust for vengeance. For when we are wronged or think that we are wronged, we are distressed, and there arises this mixture of desire and anger.

There are three forms of anger: rage, which the Greeks also call χολή or χόλος, μῆνις and κότος . When anger arises and begins to be roused, it is called rage or χολή or χόλος . Wrath again implies that the bile endures, that is to say, that the memory of the wrong abides: and indeed the Greek word for it, μῆνις is derived from μένειν, and means what abides and is transferred to memory. Rancour, on the other hand, implies watching for a suitable moment for revenge, and the Greek word for it is κότος from κεῖσθαι .

Anger further is the satellite of reason, the vindicator of desire. For when we long after anything and are opposed in our desire by some one, we are angered at that person, as though we had been wronged: and reason evidently deems that there are just grounds for displeasure in what has happened, in the case of those who, like us, have in the natural course of things to guard their own position.

Chapter 17. Concerning Imagination.

Imagination is a faculty of the unreasoning part of the soul. It is through the organs of sense that it is brought into action, and it is spoken of as sensation. And further, what is imagined and perceived is that which comes within the scope of the faculty of imagination and sensation. For example, the sense of sight is the visual faculty itself, but the object of sight is that which comes within the scope of the sense of sight, such as a stone or any other such object. Further, an imagination is an affection of the unreasoning part of the soul which is occasioned by some object acting upon the sensation. But an appearance is an empty affection of the unreasoning part of the soul, not occasioned by any object acting upon the sensation. Moreover the organ of imagination is the anterior ventricle of the brain.

Chapter 18. Concerning Sensation.

Sensation is that faculty of the soul whereby material objects can be apprehended or discriminated. And the sensoria are the organs or members through which sensations are conveyed. And the objects of sense are the things that come within the province of sensation. And lastly, the subject of sense is the living animal which possesses the faculty of sensation. Now there are five senses, and likewise five organs of sense.

The first sense is sight: and the sensoria or organs of sight are the nerves of the brain and the eyes. Now sight is primarily perception of color, but along with the color it discriminates the body that has color, and its size and form, and locality, and the intervening space and the number : also whether it is in motion or at rest, rough or smooth, even or uneven, sharp or blunt, and finally whether its composition is watery or earthy, that is, wet or dry.

The second sense is hearing, whereby voices and sounds are perceived. And it distinguishes these as sharp or deep, or smooth or loud. Its organs are the soft nerves of the brain, and the structure of the ears. Further, man and the ape are the only animals that do not move their ears.

The third sense is smell, which is caused by the nostrils transmitting the vapours to the brain: and it is bounded by the extreme limits of the anterior ventricle of the brain. It is the faculty by which vapours are perceived and apprehended. Now, the most generic distinction between vapours is whether they have a good or an evil odour, or form an intermediate class with neither a good nor an evil odour. A good odour is produced by the thorough digestion in the body of the humours. When they are only moderately digested the intermediate class is formed, and when the digestion is very imperfect or utterly wanting, an evil odour results.

The fourth sense is taste: it is the faculty whereby the humours are apprehended or perceived, and its organs of sense are the tongue, and more especially the lips, and the palate (which the Greeks call οὐρανίσκος), and in these are nerves that come from the brain and are spread out, and convey to the dominant part of the soul the perception or sensation they have encountered. The so-called gustatory qualities of the humours are these:— sweetness, pungency, bitterness, astringency, acerbity, sourness, saltness, fattiness, stickiness; for taste is capable of discriminating all these. But water has none of these qualities, and is therefore devoid of taste. Moreover, astringency is only a more intense and exaggerated form of acerbity.

The fifth sense is touch, which is common to all living things. Its organs are nerves which come from the brain and ramify all through the body. Hence the body as a whole, including even the other organs of sense, possesses the sense of touch. Within its scope come heat and cold, softness and hardness, viscosity and brittleness , heaviness and lightness: for it is by touch alone that these qualities are discriminated. On the other hand, roughness and smoothness, dryness and wetness, thickness and thinness, up and down, place and size, whenever that is such as to be embraced in a single application of the sense of touch, are all common to touch and sight, as well as denseness and rareness, that is porosity, and rotundity if it is small, and some other shapes. In like manner also by the aid of memory and thought perception of the nearness of a body is possible, and similarly perception of number up to two or three, and such small and easily reckoned figures. But it is by sight rather than touch that these things are perceived.

The Creator, it is to be noted, fashioned all the other organs of sense in pairs, so that if one were destroyed, the other might fill its place. For there are two eyes, two ears, two orifices of the nose, and two tongues, which in some animals, such as snakes, are separate, but in others, like man, are united. But touch is spread over the whole body with the exception of bones, nerves, nails, horns, hairs, ligaments, and other such structures.

Further, it is to be observed that sight is possible only in straight lines, whereas smell and hearing are not limited to straight lines only, but act in all directions. Touch, again, and taste act neither in straight lines, nor in every direction, but only when each comes near to the sensible objects that are proper to it.

Chapter 19. Concerning Thought.

The faculty of thought deals with judgments and assents, and impulse to action and disinclinations, and escapes from action: and more especially with thoughts connected with what is thinkable, and the virtues and the different branches of learning, and the theories of the arts and matters of counsel and choice. Further, it is this faculty which prophesies the future to us in dreams, and this is what the Pythagoreans, adopting the Hebrew view, hold to be the one true form of prophecy. The organ of thought then is the mid-ventricle of the brain, and the vital spirit it contains.

Chapter 20. Concerning Memory.

The faculty of memory is the cause and storehouse of remembrance and recollection. For memory is a fantasy that is left behind of some sensation and thought manifesting itself in action; or the preservation of a sensation and thought. For the soul comprehends objects of sense through the organs of sense, that is to say, it perceives, and thence arises a notion: and similarly it comprehends the objects of thought through the mind, and thence arises a thought. It is then the preservation of the types of these notions and thoughts that is spoken of as memory.

Further, it is worthy of remark that the apprehension of matters of thought depends on learning, or natural process of thought, and not on sensation. For though objects of sense are retained in the memory by themselves, only such objects of thought are remembered as we have learned, and we have no memory of their essence.

Recollection is the name given to the recovery of some memory lost by forgetfulness. For forgetfulness is just loss of memory. The faculty of imagination then, having apprehended material objects through the senses, transmits this to the faculty of thought or reason (for they are both the same), and this after it has received and passed judgment on it, passes it on to the faculty of memory. Now the organ of memory is the posterior ventricle of the brain, which the Greeks call the παρεγκεφαλίς, and the vital spirit it contains.

Chapter 21. Concerning Conception and Articulation.

Again the reasoning part of the soul is divided into conception and articulation. Conception is an activity of the soul originating in the reason without resulting in utterance. Accordingly, often, even when we are silent we run through a whole speech in our minds, and hold discussions in our dreams. And it is this faculty chiefly which constitutes us all reasoning beings. For those who are dumb by birth or have lost their voice through some disease or injury, are just as much reasoning beings. But articulation by voice or in the different dialects requires energy: that is to say, the word is articulated by the tongue and mouth, and this is why it is named articulation. It is, indeed, the messenger of thought, and it is because of it that we are called speaking beings.

Chapter 22. Concerning Passion and Energy.

Passion is a word with various meanings. It is used in regard to the body, and refers to diseases and wounds, and again, it is used in reference to the soul, and means desire and anger. But to speak broadly and generally, passion is an animal affection which is succeeded by pleasure and pain. For pain succeeds passion, but is not the same thing as passion. For passion is an affection of things without sense, but not so pain. Pain then is not passion, but the sensation of passion: and it must be considerable, that is to say, it must be great enough to come within the scope of sense.

Again, the definition of passions of the soul is this: Passion is a sensible activity of the appetitive faculty, depending on the presentation to the mind of something good or bad. Or in other words, passion is an irrational activity of the soul, resulting from the notion of something good or bad. For the notion of something good results in desire, and the notion of something bad results in anger. But passion considered as a class, that is, passion in general, is defined as a movement in one thing caused by another. Energy, on the other hand, is a drastic movement, and by drastic is meant that which is moved of itself. Thus, anger is the energy manifested by the part of the soul where anger resides, whereas passion involves the two divisions of the soul, and in addition the whole body when it is forcibly impelled to action by anger. For there has been caused movement in one thing caused by another, and this is called passion.

But in another sense energy is spoken of as passion. For energy is a movement in harmony with nature, whereas passion is a movement at variance with nature. According, then, to this view, energy may be spoken of as passion when it does not act in accord with nature, whether its movement is due to itself or to some other thing. Thus, in connection with the heart, its natural pulsation is energy, whereas its palpitation, which is an excessive and unnatural movement, is passion and not energy.

But it is not every activity of the passionate part of the soul that is called passion, but only the more violent ones, and such as are capable of causing sensation: for the minor and unperceived movements are certainly not passions. For to constitute passion there is necessary a considerable degree of force, and thus it is on this account that we add to the definition of passion that it is a sensible activity. For the lesser activities escape the notice of the senses, and do not cause passion.

Observe also that our soul possesses twofold faculties, those of knowledge, and those of life. The faculties of knowledge are mind, thought, notion, presentation, sensation: and the vital or appetitive faculties are will and choice. Now, to make what has been said clearer, let us consider these things more closely, and first let us take the faculties of knowledge.

Presentation and sensation then have already been sufficiently discussed above. It is sensation that causes a passion, which is called presentation, to arise in the soul, and from presentation comes notion. Thereafter thought, weighing the truth or falseness of the notion, determines what is true: and this explains the Greek word for thought, διάνοια, which is derived from διανοεῖν, meaning to think and discriminate. That, however, which is judged 1 Corinthians 1:10 and determined to be true, is spoken of as mind.

Or to put it otherwise: The primary activity of the mind, observe, is intelligence, but intelligence applied to any object is called a thought, and when this persists and makes on the mind an impression of the object of thought, it is named reflection, and when reflection dwells on the same object and puts itself to the test, and closely examines the relation of the thought to the soul, it gets the name prudence. Further, prudence, when it extends its area forms the power of reasoning, and is called conception, and this is defined as the fullest activity of the soul, arising in that part where reason resides, and being devoid of outward expression: and from it proceeds the uttered word spoken by the tongue. And now that we have discussed the faculties of knowledge, let us turn to the vital or appetitive faculties.

It should be understood that there is implanted in the soul by nature a faculty of desiring that which is in harmony with its nature, and of maintaining in close union all that belongs essentially to its nature: and this power is called will or θέλησις . For the essence both of existence and of living yearns after activity both as regards mind and sense, and in this it merely longs to realise its own natural and perfect being. And so this definition also is given of this natural will: will is an appetite, both rational and vital, depending only on what is natural. So that will is nothing else than the natural and vital and rational appetite of all things that go to constitute nature, that is, just the simple faculty. For the appetite of creatures without reason, since it is irrational, is not called will.

Again βούλησις or wish is a sort of natural will, that is to say, a natural and rational appetite for some definite thing. For there is seated in the soul of man a faculty of rational desire. When, then, this rational desire directs itself naturally to some definite object it is called wish. For wish is rational desire and longing for some definite thing.

Wish, however, is used both in connection with what is within our power, and in connection with what is outside our power, that is, both with regard to the possible and the impossible. For we wish often to indulge lust or to be temperate, or to sleep and the like, and these are within our power to accomplish, and possible. But we wish also to be kings, and this is not within our power, or we wish perchance never to die, and this is an impossibility.

The wish , then, has reference to the end alone, and not to the means by which the end is attained. The end is the object of our wish, for instance, to be a king or to enjoy good health: but the means by which the end is attained, that is to say, the manner in which we ought to enjoy good health, or reach the rank of king, are the objects of deliberation. Then after wish follow inquiry and speculation (ζήτησις and σκέψις), and after these, if the object is anything within our power, comes counsel or deliberation (βουλή or βούλευσις): counsel is an appetite for investigating lines of action lying within our own power. For one deliberates, whether one ought to prosecute any matter or not, and next, one decides which is the better, and this is called judgment (κρίσις). Thereafter, one becomes disposed to and forms a liking for that in favour of which deliberation gave judgment, and this is called inclination (γνώμη). For should one form a judgment and not be disposed to or form a liking for the object of that judgment, it is not called inclination. Then, again, after one has become so disposed, choice or selection (προαίρεσις and ἐπιλογή) comes into play. For choice consists in the choosing and selecting of one of two possibilities in preference to the other. Then one is impelled to action, and this is called impulse (ὁρμή): and thereafter it is brought into employment, and this is called use (χρῆσις). The last stage after we have enjoyed the use is cessation from desire.

In the case, however, of creatures without reason, as soon as appetite is roused for anything, straightway arises impulse to action. For the appetite of creatures without reason is irrational, and they are ruled by their natural appetite. Hence, neither the names of will or wish are applicable to the appetite of creatures without reason. For will is rational, free and natural desire, and in the case of man, endowed with reason as he is, the natural appetite is ruled rather than rules. For his actions are free, and depend upon reason, since the faculties of knowledge and life are bound up together in man. He is free in desire, free in wish, free in examination and investigation, free in deliberation, free in judgment, free in inclination, free in choice, free in impulse, and free in action where that is in accordance with nature.

But in the case of God , it is to be remembered, we speak of wish, but it is not correct to speak of choice. For God does not deliberate, since that is a mark of ignorance, and no one deliberates about what he knows. But if counsel is a mark of ignorance, surely choice must also be so. God, then, since He has absolute knowledge of everything, does not deliberate.

Nor in the case of the soul of the Lord do we speak of counsel or choice, seeing that He had no part in ignorance. For, although He was of a nature that is not cognisant of the future, yet because of His oneness in subsistence with God the Word, He had knowledge of all things, and that not by grace, but, as we have said, because He was one in subsistence. For He Himself was both God and Man, and hence He did not possess the will that acts by opinion or disposition. While He did possess the natural and simple will which is to be observed equally in all the personalities of men, His holy soul had not opinion (or, disposition) that is to say, no inclination opposed to His divine will, nor anything else contrary to His divine will. For opinion (or, disposition) differs as persons differ, except in the case of the holy and simple and uncompound and indivisible Godhead. There, indeed, since the subsistences are in nowise divided or separated, neither is the object of will divided. And there, since there is but one nature, there is also but one natural will. And again, since the subsistences are unseparated, the three subsistences have also one object of will, and one activity. In the case of men, however, seeing that their nature is one, their natural will is also one, but since their subsistences are separated and divided from each other, alike in place and time, and disposition to things, and in many other respects, for this reason their acts of will and their opinions are different. But in the case of our Lord Jesus Christ, since He possesses different natures, His natural wills, that is, His volitional faculties belonging to Him as God and as Man are also different. But since the subsistence is one, and He Who exercises the will is one, the object of the will, that is, the gnomic will , is also one, His human will evidently following His divine will, and willing that which the divine will willed it to will.

Further note, that will (θέλησις) and wish (βούλησις) are two different things: also the object of will (τὸ θελητόν) and the capacity for will (θελητικόν), and the subject that exercises will (ὁ θέλων), are all different. For will is just the simple faculty of willing, whereas wish is will directed to some definite object. Again, the object of will is the matter underlying the will, that is to say, the thing that we will: for instance, when appetite is roused for food. The appetite pure and simple, however, is a rational will. The capacity for will, moreover, means that which possesses the volitional faculty, for example, man. Further, the subject that exercises will is the actual person who makes use of will.

The word τὸ θελήμα, it is well to note, sometimes denotes the will, that is, the volitional faculty, and in this sense we speak of natural will: and sometimes it denotes the object of will, and we speak of will (θέλημα γνωμικόν) depending on inclination.

Chapter 23. Concerning Energy.

All the faculties we have already discussed, both those of knowledge and those of life, both the natural and the artificial, are, it is to be noted, called energies. For energy is the natural force and activity of each essence: or again, natural energy is the activity innate in every essence: and so, clearly, things that have the same essence have also the same energy, and things that have different natures have also different energies. For no essence can be devoid of natural energy.

Natural energy again is the force in each essence by which its nature is made manifest. And again: natural energy is the primal, eternally-moving force of the intelligent soul: that is, the eternally-moving word of the soul, which ever springs naturally from it. And yet again: natural energy is the force and activity of each essence which only that which is not lacks.

But actions are also called energies: for instance, speaking, eating, drinking, and such like. The natural affections also are often called energies, for instance, hunger, thirst, and so forth. And yet again, the result of the force is also often called energy.

Things are spoken of in a twofold way as being potential and actual. For we say that the child at the breast is a potential scholar, for he is so equipped that, if taught, he will become a scholar. Further, we speak of a potential and an actual scholar, meaning that the latter is versed in letters, while the former has the power of interpreting letters, but does not put it into actual use: again, when we speak of an actual scholar, we mean that he puts his power into actual use, that is to say, that he really interprets writings.

It is, therefore, to be observed that in the second sense potentiality and actuality go together; for the scholar is in the one case potential, and in the other actual.

The primal and only true energy of nature is the voluntary or rational and independent life which constitutes our humanity. I know not how those who rob the Lord of this can say that He became man.

Energy is drastic activity of nature: and by drastic is meant that which is moved of itself.

Chapter 24. Concerning what is Voluntary and what is Involuntary.

The voluntary implies a certain definite action, and so-called involuntariness also implies a certain definite action. Further, many attribute true involuntariness not only to suffering, but even to action. We must then understand action to be rational energy. Actions are followed by praise or blame, and some of them are accompanied with pleasure and others with pain; some are to be desired by the actor, others are to be shunned: further, of those that are desirable, some are always so, others only at some particular time. And so it is also with those that are to be shunned. Again, some actions enlist pity and are pardonable, others are hateful and deserve punishment. Voluntariness, then, is assuredly followed by praise or blame, and renders the action pleasurable and desirable to the actor, either for all time or for the moment of its performance. Involuntariness, on the other hand, brings merited pity or pardon in its train, and renders the act painful and undesirable to the doer, and makes him leave it in a state of incompleteness even though force is brought to bear upon him.

Further, what is involuntary, depends in part on force and in part on ignorance. It depends on force when the creative beginning in cause is from without, that is to say, when one is forced by another without being at all persuaded, or when one does not contribute to the act on one's own impulse, or does not co-operate at all, or do on one's own account that which is exacted by force. Thus we may give this definition: An involuntary act is one in which the beginning is from without, and where one does not contribute at all on one's own impulse to that which one is forced. And by beginning we mean the creative cause. All involuntary act depends, on the other hand, on ignorance, when one is not the cause of the ignorance one's self, but events just so happen. For, if one commits murder while drunk, it is an act of ignorance, but yet not involuntary : for one was one's self responsible for the cause of the ignorance, that is to say, the drunkenness. But if while shooting at the customary range one slew one's father who happened to be passing by, this would be termed an ignorant and involuntary act.

As, then, that which is involuntary is in two parts, one depending on force, the other on ignorance, that which is voluntary is the opposite of both. For that which is voluntary is the result neither of force nor of ignorance. A voluntary act, then, is one of which the beginning or cause originates in an actor, who knows each individual circumstance through which and in which the action takes place. By individual is meant what the rhetoricians call circumstantial elements: for instance, the actor, the sufferer, the action (perchance a murder), the instrument, the place, the time, the manner, the reason of the action.

Notice that there are certain things that occupy a place intermediate between what is voluntary and what is involuntary. Although they are unpleasant and painful we welcome them as the escape from a still greater trouble; for instance, to escape shipwreck we cast the cargo overboard.

Notice also that children and irrational creatures perform voluntary actions, but these do not involve the exercise of choice: further, all our actions that are done in anger and without previous deliberation are voluntary actions, but do not in the least involve free choice. Also, if a friend suddenly appears on the scene, or if one unexpectedly lights on a treasure, so far as we are concerned it is quite voluntary, but there is no question of choice in the matter. For all these things are voluntary, because we desire pleasure from them, but they do not by any means imply choice, because they are not the result of deliberation. And deliberation must assuredly precede choice, as we have said above.

Chapter 25. Concerning what is in our own power, that is, concerning Free-will.

The first enquiry involved in the consideration of free-will, that is, of what is in our own power, is whether anything is in our power : for there are many who deny this. The second is, what are the things that are in our power, and over what things do we have authority? The third is, what is the reason for which God Who created us endued us with free-will? So then we shall take up the first question, and firstly we shall prove that of those things which even our opponents grant, some are within our power. And let us proceed thus.

Of all the things that happen, the cause is said to be either God, or necessity, or fate, or nature, or chance, or accident. But God's function has to do with essence and providence: necessity deals with the movement of things that ever keep to the same course: fate with the necessary accomplishment of the things it brings to pass (for fate itself implies necessity): nature with birth, growth, destruction, plants and animals; chance with what is rare and unexpected. For chance is defined as the meeting and concurrence of two causes, originating in choice but bringing to pass something other than what is natural: for example, if a man finds a treasure while digging a ditch : for the man who hid the treasure did not do so that the other might find it, nor did the finder dig with the purpose of finding the treasure: but the former hid it that he might take it away when he wished, and the other's aim was to dig the ditch: whereas something happened quite different from what both had in view. Accident again deals with casual occurrences that take place among lifeless or irrational things, apart from nature and art. This then is their doctrine. Under which, then, of these categories are we to bring what happens through the agency of man, if indeed man is not the cause and beginning of action ? For it would not be right to ascribe to God actions that are sometimes base and unjust: nor may we ascribe these to necessity, for they are not such as ever continue the same: nor to fate, for fate implies not possibility only but necessity: nor to nature, for nature's province is animals and plants: nor to chance, for the actions of men are not rare and unexpected: nor to accident, for that is used in reference to the casual occurrences that take place in the world of lifeless and irrational things. We are left then with this fact, that the man who acts and makes is himself the author of his own works, and is a creature endowed with free-will.

Further, if man is the author of no action, the faculty of deliberation is quite superfluous: for to what purpose could deliberation be put if man is the master of none of his actions? For all deliberation is for the sake of action. But to prove that the fairest and most precious of man's endowments is quite superfluous would be the height of absurdity. If then man deliberates, he deliberates with a view to action. For all deliberation is with a view to and on account of action.

Chapter 26. Concerning Events.

Of events , some are in our hands, others are not. Those then are in our hands which we are free to do or not to do at our will, that is all actions that are done voluntarily (for those actions are not called voluntary the doing of which is not in our hands), and in a word, all that are followed by blame or praise and depend on motive and law. Strictly all mental and deliberative acts are in our hands. Now deliberation is concerned with equal possibilities: and an 'equal possibility' is an action that is itself within our power and its opposite, and our mind makes choice of the alternatives, and this is the origin of action. The actions, therefore, that are in our hands are these equal possibilities: e.g. to be moved or not to be moved, to hasten or not to hasten, to long for unnecessaries or not to do so, to tell lies or not to tell lies, to give or not to give, to rejoice or not to rejoice as fits the occasion, and all such actions as imply virtue or vice in their performance, for we are free to do or not to do these at our pleasure. Amongst equal possibilities also are included the arts, for we have it in our power to cultivate these or not as we please.

Note, however, that while the choice of what is to be done is ever in our power, the action itself often is prevented by some dispensation of the divine Providence.

Chapter 27. Concerning the reason of our endowment with Free-will.

We hold, therefore, that free-will comes on the scene at the same moment as reason, and that change and alteration are congenital to all that is produced.

For all that is produced is also subject to change. For those things must be subject to change whose production has its origin in change. And change consists in being brought into being out of nothing, and in transforming a substratum of matter into something different. Inanimate things, then, and things without reason undergo the aforementioned bodily changes, while the changes of things endowed with reason depend on choice. For reason consists of a speculative and a practical part. The speculative part is the contemplation of the nature of things, and the practical consists in deliberation and defines the true reason for what is to be done. The speculative side is called mind or wisdom, and the practical side is called reason or prudence. Every one, then, who deliberates does so in the belief that the choice of what is to be done lies in his hands, that he may choose what seems best as the result of his deliberation, and having chosen may act upon it. And if this is so, free-will must necessarily be very closely related to reason. For either man is an irrational being, or, if he is rational, he is master of his acts and endowed with free-will. Hence also creatures without reason do not enjoy free-will: for nature leads them rather than they nature, and so they do not oppose the natural appetite, but as soon as their appetite longs after anything they rush headlong after it. But man, being rational, leads nature rather than nature him, and so when he desires anything he has the power to curb his appetite or to indulge it as he pleases. Hence also creatures devoid of reason are the subjects neither of praise nor blame, while man is the subject of both praise and blame.

Note also that the angels, being rational, are endowed with free-will, and, inasmuch as they are created, are liable to change. This in fact is made plain by the devil who, although made good by the Creator, became of his own free-will the inventor of evil, and by the powers who revolted with him , that is the demons, and by the other troops of angels who abode in goodness.

Chapter 28. Concerning what is not in our hands.

Of things that are not in our hands some have their beginning or cause in those that are in our power, that is to say, the recompenses of our actions both in the present and in the age to come, but all the rest are dependent on the divine will. For the origin of all things is from God, but their destruction has been introduced by our wickedness for our punishment or benefit. For God did not create death, neither does He take delight in the destruction of living things. Wisdom 1:13 But death is the work rather of man, that is, its origin is in Adam's transgression, in like manner as all other punishments. But all other things must be referred to God. For our birth is to be referred to His creative power; and our continuance to His conservative power; and our government and safety to His providential power; and the eternal enjoyment of good things by those who preserve the laws of nature in which we are formed is to be ascribed to His goodness. But since some deny the existence of Providence, let us further devote a few words to the discussion of Providence.

Chapter 29. Concerning Providence.

Providence, then, is the care that God takes over existing things. And again: Providence is the will of God through which all existing things receive their fitting issue. But if Providence is God's will, according to true reasoning all things that come into being through Providence must necessarily be both most fair and most excellent, and such that they cannot be surpassed. For the same person must of necessity be creator of and provider for what exists: for it is not meet nor fitting that the creator of what exists and the provider should be separate persons. For in that case they would both assuredly be deficient, the one in creating, the other in providing. God therefore is both Creator and Provider, and His creative and preserving and providing power is simply His good-will. For *whatsoever the Lord pleased that did He in heaven and in earth* , and *no one resisted His will*. Romans 9:19 He willed that all things should be and they were. He wills the universe to be framed and it is framed, and all that He wills comes to pass.

That He provides, and that He provides excellently , one can most readily perceive thus. God alone is good and wise by nature. Since then He is good, He provides: for he who does not provide is not good. For even men and creatures without reason provide for their own offspring according to their nature, and he who does not provide is blamed. Again, since He is wise, He takes the best care over what exists.

When, therefore, we give heed to these things we ought to be filled with wonder at all the works of Providence, and praise them all , and accept them all without enquiry, even though they are in the eyes of many unjust, because the Providence of God is beyond our ken and comprehension, while our reasonings and actions and the future are revealed to His eyes alone. And by all I mean those that are not in our hands: for those that are in our power are outside the sphere of Providence and within that of our Free-will.

Now the works of Providence are partly according to the good-will (of God) and partly according to permission. Works of good-will include all those that are undeniably good, while works of permission are....... For Providence often permits the just man to encounter misfortune in order that he may reveal to others the virtue that lies concealed within him , as was the case with Job. Job 1:11 At other times it allows something strange to be done in order that something great and marvellous might be accomplished through the seemingly-strange act, as when the salvation of men was brought about through the Cross. In another way it allows the pious man to suffer sore trials in order that he may not depart from a right conscience nor lapse into pride on account of the power and grace granted to him, as was the case with Paul 2 Corinthians 2:7 .

One man is forsaken for a season with a view to another's restoration, in order that others when they see his state may be taught a lesson , as in the case of Lazarus and the rich man. Luke 16:19 For it belongs to our nature to be cast down when we see persons in distress. Another is deserted by Providence in order that another may be glorified, and not for his own sin or that of his parents, just as the man who was blind from his birth ministered to the glory of the Son of Man. John 9:1 Again another is permitted to suffer in order to stir up emulation in the breasts of others, so that others by magnifying the glory of the sufferer may resolutely welcome suffering in the hope of future glory and the desire for future blessings, as in the case of the martyrs. Another is allowed to fall at times into some act of baseness in order that another worse fault may be thus corrected, as for instance when God allows a man who takes pride in his virtue and righteousness to fall away into fornication in order that he may be brought through this fall into the perception of his own weakness and be humbled and approach and make confession to the Lord.

Moreover, it is to be observed that the choice of what is to be done is in our own hands : but the final issue depends, in the one case when our actions are good, on the cooperation of God, Who in His justice brings help according to His foreknowledge to such as choose the good with a right conscience, and, in the other case when our actions are to evil, on the desertion by God, Who again in His justice stands aloof in accordance with His foreknowledge.

Now there are two forms of desertion: for there is desertion in the matters of guidance and training, and there is complete and hopeless desertion. The former has in view the restoration and safety and glory of the sufferer, or the rousing of feelings of emulation and imitation in others, or the glory of God: but the latter is when man, after God has done all that was possible to save him, remains of his own set purpose blind and uncured, or rather incurable, and then he is handed over to utter destruction, as was Judas. Matthew 26:24 May God be gracious to us, and deliver us from such desertion.

Observe further that the ways of God's providence are many, and they cannot be explained in words nor conceived by the mind.

And remember that all the assaults of dark and evil fortune contribute to the salvation of those who receive them with thankfulness, and are assuredly ambassadors of help.

Also one must bear in mind that God's original wish was that all should be saved and come to His Kingdom. 1 Timothy 2:4 For it was not for punishment that He formed us but to share in His goodness, inasmuch as He is a good God. But inasmuch as He is a just God, His will is that sinners should suffer punishment.

The first then is called God's antecedent will and pleasure, and springs from Himself, while the second is called God's consequent will and permission, and has its origin in us. And the latter is two-fold; one part dealing with matters of guidance and training, and having in view our salvation, and the other being hopeless and leading to our utter punishment, as we said above. And this is the case with actions that are not left in our hands.

But of actions that are in our hands the good ones depend on His antecedent goodwill and pleasure, while the wicked ones depend neither on His antecedent nor on His consequent will, but are a concession to free-will. For that which is the result of compulsion has neither reason nor virtue in it. God makes provision for all creation and makes all creation the instrument of His help and training, yea often even the demons themselves, as for example in the cases of Job and the swine.

Chapter 30. Concerning Prescience and Predestination.

We ought to understand that while God knows all things beforehand, yet He does not predetermine all things. For He knows beforehand those things that are in our power, but He does not predetermine them. For it is not His will that there should be wickedness nor does He choose to compel virtue. So that predetermination is the work of the divine command based on foreknowledge. But on the other hand God predetermines those things which are not within our power in accordance with His prescience. For already God in His prescience has prejudged all things in accordance with His goodness and justice.

Bear in mind, too , that virtue is a gift from God implanted in our nature, and that He Himself is the source and cause of all good, and without His co-operation and help we cannot will or do any good thing. But we have it in our power either to abide in virtue and follow God, Who calls us into ways of virtue, or to stray from paths of virtue, which is to dwell in wickedness, and to follow the devil who summons but cannot compel us. For wickedness is nothing else than the withdrawal of goodness, just as darkness is nothing else than the withdrawal of light. While then we abide in the natural state we abide in virtue, but when we deviate from the natural state, that is from virtue, we come into an unnatural state and dwell in wickedness.

Repentance is the returning from the unnatural into the natural state, from the devil to God, through discipline and effort.

Man then the Creator made male, giving him to share in His own divine grace, and bringing him thus into communion with Himself: and thus it was that he gave in the manner of a prophet the names to living things, with authority as though they were given to be his slaves. For having been endowed with reason and mind, and free-will after the image of God, he was fitly entrusted with dominion over earthly things by the common Creator and Master of all.

But since God in His prescience knew that man would transgress and become liable to destruction, He made from him a female to be a help to him like himself; a help, indeed, for the conservation of the race after the transgression from age to age by generation. For the earliest formation is called 'making' and not 'generation.' For 'making' is the original formation at God's hands, while 'generation' is the succession from each other made necessary by the sentence of death imposed on us on account of the transgression.

This man He placed in Paradise, a home that was alike spiritual and sensible. For he lived in the body on the earth in the realm of sense, while he dwelt in the spirit among the angels, cultivating divine thoughts, and being supported by them: living in naked simplicity a life free from artificiality, and being led up through His creations to the one and only Creator, in Whose contemplation he found joy and gladness.

When therefore He had furnished his nature with free-will, He imposed a law on him, not to taste of the tree of knowledge. Concerning this tree, we have said as much as is necessary in the chapter about Paradise, at least as much as it was in our power to say. And with this command He gave the promise that, if he should preserve the dignity of the soul by giving the victory to reason, and acknowledging his Creator and observing His command, he should share eternal blessedness and live to all eternity, proving mightier than death: but if forsooth he should subject the soul to the body, and prefer the delights of the body, comparing himself in ignorance of his true dignity to the senseless beasts , and shaking off His Creator's yoke, and neglecting His divine injunction, he will be liable to death and corruption, and will be compelled to labour throughout a miserable life. For it was no profit to man to obtain incorruption while still untried and unproved, lest he should fall into pride and under the judgment of the devil. For through his incorruption the devil, when he had fallen as the result of his own free choice, was firmly established in wickedness, so that there was no room for repentance and no hope of change: just as, moreover, the angels also, when they had made free choice of virtue became through grace immoveably rooted in goodness.

It was necessary, therefore, that man should first be put to the test (for man untried and unproved would be worth nothing), and being made perfect by the trial through the observance of the command should thus receive incorruption as the prize of his virtue. For being intermediate between God and matter he was destined, if he kept the command, to be delivered from his natural relation to existing things and to be made one with God's estate, and to be immoveably established in goodness, but, if he transgressed and inclined the rather to what was material, and tore his mind from the Author of his being, I mean God, his fate was to be corruption, and he was to become subject to passion instead of passionless, and mortal instead of immortal, and dependent on connection and unsettled generation. And in his desire for life he would cling to pleasures as though they were necessary to maintain it, and would fearlessly abhor those who sought to deprive him of these, and transfer his desire from God to matter, and his anger from the real enemy of his salvation to his own brethren. The envy of the devil then was the reason of man's fall. For that same demon, so full of envy and with such a hatred of good, would not suffer us to enjoy the pleasures of heaven, when he himself was kept below on account of his arrogance, and hence the false one tempts miserable man with the hope of Godhead, and leading him up to as great a height of arrogance as himself, he hurls him down into a pit of destruction just as deep.

BOOK III

Chapter 1. Concerning the Divine Œconomy and God's care over us, and concerning our salvation.

Man, then, was thus snared by the assault of the arch-fiend, and broke his Creator's command, and was stripped of grace and put off his confidence with God, and covered himself with the asperities of a toilsome life (for this is the meaning of the fig-leaves); and was clothed about with death, that is, mortality and the grossness of flesh (for this is what the garment of skins signifies); and was banished from Paradise by God's just judgment, and condemned to death, and made subject to corruption. Yet, notwithstanding all this, in His pity, God, Who gave him his being, and Who in His graciousness bestowed on him a life of happiness, did not disregard man. But He first trained him in many ways and called him back, by groans and trembling, by the deluge of water, and the utter destruction of almost the whole race Genesis 6:13, by confusion and diversity of tongues , by the rule of angels , by the burning of cities , by figurative manifestations of God, by wars and victories and defeats, by signs and wonders, by manifold faculties, by the law and the prophets: for by all these means God earnestly strove to emancipate man from the wide-spread and enslaving bonds of sin, which had made life such a mass of iniquity, and to effect man's return to a life of happiness. For it was sin that brought death like a wild and savage beast into the world Wisdom 2:24 to the ruin of the human life. But it behooved the Redeemer to be without sin, and not made liable through sin to death, and further, that His nature should be strengthened and renewed, and trained by labour and taught the way of virtue which leads away from corruption to the life eternal and, in the end, is revealed the mighty ocean of love to man that is about Him. For the very Creator and Lord Himself undertakes a struggle in behalf of the work of His own hands, and learns by toil to become Master. And since the enemy snares man by the hope of Godhead, he himself is snared in turn by the screen of flesh, and so are shown at once the goodness and wisdom, the justice and might of God. God's goodness is revealed in that He did not disregard the frailty of His own handiwork, but was moved with compassion for him in his fall, and stretched forth His hand to him: and His justice in that when man was overcome He did not make another victorious over the tyrant, nor did He snatch man by might from death, but in His goodness and justice He made him, who had become through his sins the slave of death, himself once more conqueror and rescued like by like, most difficult though it seemed: and His wisdom is seen in His devising the most fitting solution of the difficulty. For by the good pleasure of our God and Father, the Only-begotten Son and Word of God and God, Who is in the bosom of the God and Father John 1:18, of like essence with the Father and the Holy Spirit, Who was before the ages, Who is without beginning and was in the beginning, Who is in the presence of the God and Father, and is God and made in the form of God Philippians 2:6, bent the heavens and descended to earth: that is to say, He humbled without humiliation His lofty station which yet could not be humbled, and condescends to His servants , with a condescension ineffable and incomprehensible: (for that is what the descent signifies). And God being perfect becomes perfect man, and brings to perfection the newest of all new things Ecclesiastes 1:10, the only new thing under the Sun, through which the boundless might of God is manifested. For what greater thing is there, than that God should become Man? And the Word became flesh without being changed, of the Holy Spirit, and Mary the holy and ever-virgin one, the mother of God. And He acts as mediator between God and man, He the only lover of man conceived in the Virgin's chaste womb without will or desire, or any connection with man or pleasurable generation, but through the Holy Spirit and the first offspring of Adam. And He becomes obedient to the Father Who is like us, and finds a remedy for our disobedience in what He had assumed from us, and became a pattern of obedience to us without which it is not possible to obtain salvation.

Chapter 2. — Concerning the manner in which the Word was conceived, and concerning His divine incarnation.

The angel of the Lord was sent to the Holy Virgin, who was descended from David's line. Luke 1:27 *For it is evident that our Lord sprang out of Judah, of which tribe no one turned his attention to the altar* Hebrews 7:14, as the divine apostle said: but about this we will speak more accurately later. And bearing glad tidings to her, he said, *Hail thou highly favoured one, the Lord is with you.* Luke 1:28 And she was troubled at his word, and the angel said to her, *Fear not, Mary, for you have found favour with God, and shall bring forth a Son and shall call His name Jesus* ; for He shall save His people from their sins. Matthew 1:21 Hence it comes that Jesus has the interpretation Saviour. And when she asked in her perplexity, *How can this be, seeing I know not a man* Luke 1:34? The angel again answered her, *The Holy Spirit shall come upon you, and the power of the Highest shall overshadow you. Therefore also that holy thing which shall be born of you shall be called the Son of God.* Luke 1:35 And she said to him, *Behold the handmaid of the Lord: be it unto me according to Your word.*

So then, after the assent of the Holy Virgin, the Holy Spirit descended on her, according to the word of the Lord which the angel spoke, purifying her , and granting her power to receive the divinity of the Word, and likewise power to bring forth. And then was she overshadowed by the enhypostatic Wisdom and Power of the most high God, the Son of God Who is of like essence with the Father as of Divine seed, and from her holy and most pure blood He formed flesh animated with the spirit of reason and thought, the first-fruits of our compound nature : not by procreation but by creation through the Holy Spirit: not developing the fashion of the body by gradual additions but perfecting it at once, He Himself, the very Word of God, standing to the flesh in the relation of subsistence. For the divine Word was not made one with flesh that had an independent pre-existence , but taking up His abode in the womb of the Holy Virgin, He unreservedly in His own subsistence took upon Himself through the pure blood of the eternal Virgin a body of flesh animated with the spirit of reason and thought, thus assuming to Himself the first-fruits of man's compound nature, Himself, the Word, having become a subsistence in the flesh. So that He is at once flesh, and at the same time flesh of God the Word, and likewise flesh animated, possessing both reason and thought. Wherefore we speak not of man as having become God, but of God as having become Man. For being by nature perfect God, He naturally became likewise perfect Man: and did not change His nature nor make the dispensation an empty show, but became, without confusion or change or division, one in subsistence with the flesh, which was conceived of the Holy Virgin, and animated with reason and thought, and had found existence in Him, while He did not change the nature of His divinity into the essence of flesh, nor the essence of flesh into the nature of His divinity, and did not make one compound nature out of His divine nature and the human nature He had assumed.

Chapter 3. Concerning Christ's two natures, in opposition to those who hold that He has only one.

For the two natures were united with each other without change or alteration, neither the divine nature departing from its native simplicity, nor yet the human being either changed into the nature of God or reduced to non-existence, nor one compound nature being produced out of the two. For the compound nature cannot be of the same essence as either of the natures out of which it is compounded, as made one thing out of others: for example, the body is composed of the four elements, but is not of the same essence as fire or air, or water or earth, nor does it keep these names. If, therefore, after the union, Christ's nature was, as the heretics hold, a compound unity, He had changed from a simple into a compound nature , and is not of the same essence as the Father Whose nature is simple, nor as the mother, who is not a compound of divinity and humanity. Nor will He then be in divinity and humanity: nor will He be called either God or Man, but simply Christ: and the word Christ will be the name not of the subsistence, but of what in their view is the one nature.

We, however, do not give it as our view that Christ's nature is compound, nor yet that He is one thing made of other things and differing from them as man is made of soul and body, or as the body is made of the four elements, but hold that, though He is constituted of these different parts He is yet the same. For we confess that He alike in His divinity and in His humanity both is and is said to be perfect God, the same Being, and that He consists of two natures, and exists in two natures. Further, by the word Christ we understand the name of the subsistence, not in the sense of one kind, but as signifying the existence of two natures. For in His own person He anointed Himself; as God anointing His body with His own divinity, and as Man being anointed. For He is Himself both God and Man. And the anointing is the divinity of His humanity. For if Christ, being of one compound nature, is of like essence to the Father, then the Father also must be compound and of like essence with the flesh, which is absurd and extremely blasphemous.

How, indeed, could one and the same nature come to embrace opposing and essential differences? For how is it possible that the same nature should be at once created and uncreated, mortal and immortal, circumscribed and uncircumscribed?

But if those who declare that Christ has only one nature should say also that that nature is a simple one, they must admit either that He is God pure and simple, and thus reduce the incarnation to a mere pretence, or that He is only man, according to Nestorius. And how then about His being perfect in divinity and perfect in humanity? And when can Christ be said to be of two natures, if they hold that He is of one composite nature after the union? For it is surely clear to every one that before the union Christ's nature was one.

But this is what leads the heretics astray, viz., that they look upon nature and subsistence as the same thing. For when we speak of the nature of men as one , observe that in saying this we are not looking to the question of soul and body. For when we compare together the soul and the body it cannot be said that they are of one nature. But since there are very many subsistences of men, and yet all have the same kind of nature : for all are composed of soul and body, and all have part in the nature of the soul, and possess the essence of the body, and the common form: we speak of the one nature of these very many and different subsistences; while each subsistence, to wit, has two natures, and fulfils itself in two natures, namely, soul and body.

But a common form cannot be admitted in the case of our Lord Jesus Christ. For neither was there ever, nor is there, nor will there ever be another Christ constituted of deity and humanity, and existing in deity and humanity at once perfect God and perfect man. And thus in the case of our Lord Jesus Christ we cannot speak of one nature made up of divinity and humanity, as we do in the case of the individual made up of soul and body. For in the latter case we have to do with an individual, but Christ is not an individual. For there is no predicable form of Christlihood, so to speak, that He possesses. And therefore we hold that there has been a union of two perfect natures, one divine and one human; not with disorder or confusion, or intermixture , or commingling, as is said by the God-accursed Dioscorus and by Eutyches and Severus, and all that impious company: and not in a personal or relative manner, or as a matter of dignity or agreement in will, or equality in honour, or identity in name, or good pleasure, as Nestorius, hated of God, said, and Diodorus and Theodorus of Mopsuestia, and their diabolical tribe: but by synthesis; that is, in subsistence, without change or confusion or alteration or difference or separation, and we confess that in two perfect natures there is but one subsistence of the Son of God incarnate ; holding that there is one and the same subsistence belonging to His divinity and His humanity, and granting that the two natures are preserved in Him after the union, but we do not hold that each is separate and by itself, but that they are united to each other in one compound subsistence. For we look upon the union as essential, that is, as true and not imaginary. We say that it is essential , moreover, not in the sense of two natures resulting in one compound nature, but in the sense of a true union of them in one compound subsistence of the Son of God, and we hold that their essential difference is preserved. For the created remains created, and the uncreated, uncreated: the mortal remains mortal; the immortal, immortal: the circumscribed, circumscribed: the uncircumscribed, uncircumscribed: the visible, visible: the invisible, invisible. The one part is all glorious with wonders: while the other is the victim of insults.

Moreover, the Word appropriates to Himself the attributes of humanity: for all that pertains to His holy flesh is His: and He imparts to the flesh His own attributes by way of communication in virtue of the interpenetration of the parts one with another, and the oneness according to subsistence, and inasmuch as He Who lived and acted both as God and as man, taking to Himself either form and holding intercourse with the other form, was one and the same. Hence it is that the Lord of Glory is said to have been crucified 1 Corinthians 2:8, although His divine nature never endured the Cross, and that the Son of Man is allowed to have been in heaven before the Passion, as the Lord Himself said. John 3:13 For the Lord of Glory is one and the same with Him Who is in nature and in truth the Son of Man, that is, Who became man, and both His wonders and His sufferings are known to us, although His wonders were worked in His divine capacity, and His sufferings endured as man. For we know that, just as is His one subsistence, so is the essential difference of the nature preserved. For how could difference be preserved if the very things that differ from one another are not preserved? For difference is the difference between things that differ. In so far as Christ's natures differ from one another, that is, in the matter of essence, we hold that Christ unites in Himself two extremes: in respect of His divinity He is connected with the Father and the Spirit, while in respect of His humanity He is connected with

His mother and all mankind. And in so far as His natures are united, we hold that He differs from the Father and the Spirit on the one hand, and from the mother and the rest of mankind on the other. For the natures are united in His subsistence, having one compound subsistence, in which He differs from the Father and the Spirit, and also from the mother and us.

Chapter 4. Concerning the manner of the Mutual Communication.

Now we have often said already that essence is one thing and subsistence another, and that essence signifies the common and general form of subsistences of the same kind, such as God, man, while subsistence marks the individual, that is to say, Father, Son, Holy Spirit, or Peter, Paul. Observe, then, that the names, divinity and humanity, denote essences or natures: while the names, God and man, are applied both in connection with natures, as when we say that God is incomprehensible essence, and that God is one, and with reference to subsistences, that which is more specific having the name of the more general applied to it, as when the Scripture says, *Therefore God, your God, has anointed you* , or again, *There was a certain man in the land of Uz* Job 1:1, for it was only to Job that reference was made.

Therefore, in the case of our Lord Jesus Christ, seeing that we recognise that He has two natures but only one subsistence compounded of both, when we contemplate His natures we speak of His divinity and His humanity, but when we contemplate the subsistence compounded of the natures we sometimes use terms that have reference to His double nature, as Christ, and at once God and man, and God Incarnate; and sometimes those that imply only one of His natures, as God alone, or Son of God, and man alone, or Son of Man; sometimes using names that imply His loftiness and sometimes those that imply His lowliness. For He Who is alike God and man is one, being the former from the Father ever without cause, but having become the latter afterwards for His love towards man.

When, then, we speak of His divinity we do not ascribe to it the properties of humanity. For we do not say that His divinity is subject to passion or created. Nor, again, do we predicate of His flesh or of His humanity the properties of divinity: for we do not say that His flesh or His humanity is uncreated. But when we speak of His subsistence, whether we give it a name implying both natures, or one that refers to only one of them, we still attribute to it the properties of both natures. For Christ, which name implies both natures, is spoken of as at once God and man, created and uncreated, subject to suffering and incapable of suffering: and when He is named Son of God and God, in reference to only one of His natures, He still keeps the properties of the co-existing nature, that is, the flesh, being spoken of as God who suffers, and as the Lord of Glory crucified 1 Corinthians 2:8, not in respect of His being God but in respect of His being at the same time man. Likewise also when He is called Man and Son of Man, He still keeps the properties and glories of the divine nature, a child before the ages, and man who knew no beginning; it is not, however, as child or man but as God that He is before the ages, and became a child in the end. And this is the manner of the mutual communication, either nature giving in exchange to the other its own properties through the identity of the subsistence and the interpenetration of the parts with one another. Accordingly we can say of Christ: *This our God was seen upon the earth and lived among men* , and *This man is uncreated and impossible and uncircumscribed.*

Chapter 5. Concerning the number of the Natures.

In the case, therefore, of the Godhead we confess that there is but one nature, but hold that there are three subsistences actually existing, and hold that all things that are of nature and essence are simple, and recognise the difference of the subsistences only in the three properties of independence of cause and Fatherhood, of dependence on cause and Sonship, of dependence on cause and procession. And we know further that these are indivisible and inseparable from each other and united into one, and interpenetrating one another without confusion. Yea, I repeat, united without confusion, for they are three although united, and they are distinct, although inseparable. For although each has an independent existence, that is to say, is a perfect subsistence and has an individuality of its own, that is, has a special mode of existence, yet they are one in essence and in the natural properties, and in being inseparable and indivisible from the Father's subsistence, and they both are and are said to be one God. In the very same way, then, in the case of the divine and ineffable dispensation , exceeding all thought and comprehension, I mean the Incarnation of the One God the Word of the Holy Trinity, and our Lord Jesus Christ, we confess that there are two natures, one divine and one human, joined together with one another and united in subsistence , so that one compound subsistence is formed out of the two natures: but we hold that the two natures are still preserved, even after the union, in the one compound subsistence, that is, in the one Christ, and that these exist in reality and have their natural properties; for they are united without confusion, and are distinguished and enumerated without being separable. And just as the three subsistences of the Holy Trinity are united without confusion, and are distinguished and enumerated without being separable , the enumeration not entailing division or separation or alienation or cleavage among them (for we recognise one God the Father, the Son and the Holy Spirit), so in the same way the natures of Christ also, although they are united, yet are united without confusion; and although they interpenetrate one another, yet they do not permit of change or transmutation of one into the other. For each keeps its own natural individuality strictly unchanged. And thus it is that they can be enumerated without the enumeration introducing division. For Christ, indeed, is one, perfect both in divinity and in humanity. For it is not the nature of number to cause separation or unity, but its nature is to indicate the quantity of what is enumerated, whether these are united or separated: for we have unity, for instance, when fifty stones compose a wall, but we have separation when the fifty stones lie on the ground; and again, we have unity when we speak of coal having two natures, namely, fire and wood, but we have separation in that the nature of fire is one thing, and the nature of wood another thing; for these things are united and separated not by number, but in another way. So, then, just as even though the three subsistences of the Godhead are united with each other, we cannot speak of them as one subsistence because we should confuse and do away with the difference between the subsistences, so also we cannot speak of the two natures of Christ as one nature, united though they are in subsistence, because we should then confuse and do away with and reduce to nothing the difference between the two natures.

Chapter 6. That in one of its subsistences the divine nature is united in its entirety to the human nature, in its entirety and not only part to part.

What is common and general is predicated of the included particulars. Essence, then, is common as being a form , while subsistence is particular. It is particular not as though it had part of the nature and had not the rest, but particular in a numerical sense, as being individual. For it is in number and not in nature that the difference between subsistences is said to lie. Essence, therefore, is predicated of subsistence, because in each subsistence of the same form the essence is perfect. Wherefore subsistences do not differ from each other in essence but in the accidents which indeed are the characteristic properties, but characteristic of subsistence and not of nature. For indeed they define subsistence as essence along with accidents. So that the subsistence contains both the general and the particular, and has an independent existence , while essence has not an independent existence but is contemplated in the subsistences. Accordingly when one of the subsistences suffers, the whole essence, being capable of suffering , is held to have suffered in one of its subsistences as much as the subsistence suffered, but it does not necessarily follow, however, that all the subsistences of the same class should suffer along with the suffering subsistence.

Thus, therefore, we confess that the nature of the Godhead is wholly and perfectly in each of its subsistences, wholly in the Father, wholly in the Son, and wholly in the Holy Spirit. Wherefore also the Father is perfect God, the Son is perfect God, and the Holy Spirit is perfect God. In like manner, too, in the Incarnation of the Trinity of the One God the Word of the Holy Trinity, we hold that in one of its subsistences the nature of the Godhead is wholly and perfectly united with the whole nature of humanity, and not part united to part. The divine Apostle in truth says that *in Him dwells all the fullness of the Godhead bodily* Colossians 2:9, that is to say in His flesh. And His divinely-inspired disciple, Dionysius, who had so deep a knowledge of things divine, said that the Godhead as a whole had fellowship with us in one of its own subsistences. But we shall not be driven to hold that all the subsistences of the Holy Godhead, to wit the three, are made one in subsistence with all the subsistences of humanity. For in no other respect did the Father and the Holy Spirit take part in the incarnation of God the Word than according to good will and pleasure. But we hold that to the whole of human nature the whole essence of the Godhead was united. For God the Word omitted none of the things which He implanted in our nature when He formed us in the beginning, but took them all upon Himself, body and soul both intelligent and rational, and all their properties. For the creature that is devoid of one of these is not man. But He in His fullness took upon Himself me in my fullness, and was united whole to whole that He might in His grace bestow salvation on the whole man. For what has not been taken cannot be healed.

The Word of God , then, was united to flesh through the medium of mind which is intermediate between the purity of God and the grossness of flesh. For the mind holds sway over soul and body, but while the mind is the purest part of the soul God is that of the mind. And when it is allowed by that which is more excellent, the mind of Christ gives proof of its own authority , but it is under the dominion of and obedient to that which is more excellent, and does those things which the divine will purposes.

Further the mind has become the seat of the divinity united with it in subsistence, just as is evidently the case with the body too, not as an inmate , which is the impious error into which the heretics fall when they say that one bushel cannot contain two bushels, for they are judging what is immaterial by material standards. How indeed could Christ be called perfect God and perfect man, and be said to be of like essence with the Father and with us, if only part of the divine nature is joined in Him to part of the human nature ?

We hold, moreover, that our nature has been raised from the dead and has ascended to the heavens and taken its seat at the right hand of the Father: not that all the persons of men have risen from the dead and taken their seat at the right hand of the Father, but that this has happened to the whole of our nature in the subsistence of Christ. Verily the divine Apostle says, *God has raised us up together and made us sit together in Christ* Ephesians 2:6 .

And this further we hold, that the union took place through common essences. For every essence is common to the subsistences contained in it, and there cannot be found a partial and particular nature, that is to say, essence: for otherwise we would have to hold that the same subsistences are at once the same and different in essence, and that the Holy Trinity in respect of the divinity is at once the same and different in essence. So then the same nature is to be observed in each of the subsistences, and when we said that the nature of the word became flesh, as did the blessed Athanasius and Cyrillus, we mean that the divinity was joined to the flesh. Hence we cannot say The nature of the Word suffered; for the divinity in it did not suffer, but we say that the human nature, not by any means, however, meaning all the subsistences of men, suffered in Christ, and we confess further that Christ suffered in His human nature. So that when we speak of the nature of the Word we mean the Word Himself. And the Word has both the general element of essence and the particular element of subsistence.

Chapter 7. Concerning the one compound subsistence of God the Word.

We hold then that the divine subsistence of God the Word existed before all else and is without time and eternal, simple and uncompound, uncreated, incorporeal, invisible, intangible, uncircumscribed, possessing all the Father possesses, since He is of the same essence with Him, differing from the Father's subsistence in the manner of His generation and the relation of the Father's subsistence, being perfect also and at no time separated from the Father's subsistence: and in these last days, without leaving the Father's bosom, took up His abode in an uncircumscribed manner in the womb of the Holy Virgin, without the instrumentality of seed, and in an incomprehensible manner known only to Himself, and causing the flesh derived from the holy Virgin to subsist in the very subsistence that was before all the ages.

So then He was both in all things and above all things and also dwelt in the womb of the holy Mother of God, but in it by the energy of the incarnation. He therefore became flesh and He took upon Himself thereby the first-fruits of our compound nature , viz., the flesh animated with the intelligent and national soul, so that the very subsistence of God the Word was changed into the subsistence of the flesh, and the subsistence of the Word, which was formerly simple, became compound , yea compounded of two perfect natures, divinity and humanity, and bearing the characteristic and distinctive property of the divine Sonship of God the Word in virtue of which it is distinguished from the Father and the Spirit, and also the characteristic and distinctive properties of the flesh, in virtue of which it differs from the Mother and the rest of mankind, bearing further the properties of the divine nature in virtue of which it is united to the Father and the Spirit, and the marks of the human nature in virtue of which it is united to the Mother and to us. And further it differs from the Father and the Spirit and the Mother and us in being at once God and man. For this we know to be the most special property of the subsistence of Christ.

Wherefore we confess Him, even after the incarnation, the one Son of God, and likewise Son of Man, one Christ, one Lord, the only-begotten Son and Word of God, one Lord Jesus. We reverence His two generations, one from the Father before time and beyond cause and reason and time and nature, and one in the end for our sake, and like to us and above us; for our sake because it was for our salvation, like to us in that He was man born of woman at full time , and above us because it was not by seed, but by the Holy Spirit and the Holy Virgin Mary , transcending the laws of parturition. We proclaim Him not as God only, devoid of our humanity, nor yet as man only, stripping Him of His divinity, nor as two distinct persons, but as one and the same, at once God and man, perfect God and perfect man, wholly God and wholly man, the same being wholly God, even though He was also flesh and wholly man, even though He was also most high God. And by perfect God and perfect man we mean to emphasize the fullness and unfailingness of the natures: while by wholly God and wholly man we mean to lay stress on the singularity and individuality of the subsistence.

And we confess also that there is one incarnate nature of God the Word, expressing by the word incarnate the essence of the flesh, according to the blessed Cyril. And so the Word was made flesh and yet did not abandon His own proper immateriality: He became wholly flesh and yet remained wholly uncircumscribed. So far as He is body He is diminished and contracted into narrow limits, but inasmuch as He is God He is uncircumscribed, His flesh not being coextensive with His uncircumscribed divinity.

He is then wholly perfect God, but yet is not simply God: for He is not only God but also man. And He is also wholly perfect man but not simply man, for He is not only man but also God. For simply here has reference to His nature, and wholly to His subsistence, just as another thing would refer to nature, while another would refer to subsistence.

But observe that although we hold that the natures of the Lord permeate one another, yet we know that the permeation springs from the divine nature. For it is that that penetrates and permeates all things, as it wills, while nothing penetrates it: and it is it, too, that imparts to the flesh its own peculiar glories, while abiding itself impossible and without participation in the affections of the flesh. For if the sun imparts to us his energies and yet does not participate in ours, how much the rather must this be true of the Creator and Lord of the Sun.

Chapter 8. In reply to those who ask whether the natures of the Lord are brought under a continuous or a discontinuous quantity.

If any one asks concerning the natures of the Lord if they are brought under a continuous or discontinuous quantity , we will say that the natures of the Lord are neither one body nor one superficies , nor one line, nor time, nor place, so as to be reduced to a continuous quantity. For these are the things that are reckoned continuously.

Further note that number deals with things that differ, and it is quite impossible to enumerate things that differ from one another in no respect: and just so far as they differ are they enumerated: for instance, Peter and Paul are not counted separately in so far as they are one. For since they are one in respect of their essence they cannot be spoken of as two natures, but as they differ in respect of subsistence they are spoken of as two subsistences. So that number deals with differences, and just as the differing objects differ from one another so far they are enumerated.

The natures of the Lord, then, are united without confusion so far as regards subsistence, and they are divided without separation according to the method and manner of difference. And it is not according to the manner in which they are united that they are enumerated, for it is not in respect of subsistence that we hold that there are two natures of Christ: but according to the manner in which they are divided without separation they are enumerated, for it is in respect of the method and manner of difference that there are two natures of Christ. For being united in subsistence and permeating one another, they are united without confusion, each preserving throughout its own peculiar and natural difference. Hence, since they are enumerated according to the manner of difference, and that alone, they must be brought under a discontinuous quantity.

Christ, therefore , is one, perfect God and perfect man: and Him we worship along with the Father and the Spirit, with one obeisance, adoring even His immaculate flesh and not holding that the flesh is not meet for worship: for in fact it is worshipped in the one subsistence of the Word, which indeed became subsistence for it. But in this we do not do homage to that which is created. For we worship Him, not as mere flesh, but as flesh united with divinity, and because His two natures are brought under the one person and one subsistence of God the Word. I fear to touch coal because of the fire bound up with the wood. I worship the twofold nature of Christ because of the divinity that is in Him bound up with flesh. For I do not introduce a fourth person into the Trinity. God forbid! But I confess one person of God the Word and of His flesh, and the Trinity remains Trinity, even after the incarnation of the Word.

In reply to those who ask whether the two natures are brought under a continuous or a discontinuous quantity.

The natures of the Lord are neither one body nor one superficies, nor one line, nor place, nor time, so as to be brought under a continuous quantity: for these are the things that are reckoned continuously. But the natures of the Lord are united without confusion in respect of subsistence, and are divided without separation according to the method and manner of difference. And according to the manner in which they are united they are not enumerated. For we do not say that the natures of Christ are two subsistences or two in respect of subsistence. But according to the manner in which they are divided without division, are they enumerated. For there are two natures according to the method and manner of difference. For being united in subsistence and permeating one another they are united without confusion, neither having been changed into the other, but each preserving its own natural difference even after the union. For that which is created remained created, and that which is uncreated, uncreated. By the manner of difference, then, and in that alone, they are enumerated, and thus are brought under discontinuous quantity. For things which differ from each other in no respect cannot be enumerated, but just so far as they differ are they enumerated; for instance, Peter and Paul are not enumerated in those respects in which they are one: for being one in respect of their essence they are not two natures nor are they so spoken of. But inasmuch as they differ in subsistence they are spoken of as two subsistences. So that difference is the cause of number.

Chapter 9. In reply to the question whether there is Nature that has no Subsistence.

For although there is no nature without subsistence, nor essence apart from person (since in truth it is in persons and subsistences that essence and nature are to be contemplated), yet it does not necessarily follow that the natures that are united to one another in subsistence should have each its own proper subsistence. For after they have come together into one subsistence, it is possible that neither should they be without subsistence, nor should each have its own peculiar subsistence, but that both should have one and the same subsistence. For since one and the same subsistence of the Word has become the subsistence of the natures, neither of them is permitted to be without subsistence, nor are they allowed to have subsistences that differ from each other, or to have sometimes the subsistence of this nature and sometimes of that, but always without division or separation they both have the same subsistence — a subsistence which is not broken up into parts or divided, so that one part should belong to this, and one to that, but which belongs wholly to this and wholly to that in its absolute entirety. For the flesh of God the Word did not subsist as an independent subsistence, nor did there arise another subsistence besides that of God the Word, but as it existed in that it became rather a subsistence which subsisted in another, than one which was an independent subsistence. Wherefore, neither does it lack subsistence altogether, nor yet is there thus introduced into the Trinity another subsistence.

Chapter 10. Concerning the Trisagium (the Thrice Holy).

This being so , we declare that the addition which the vain-minded Peter the Fuller made to the Trisagium or Thrice Holy Hymn is blasphemous ; for it introduces a fourth person into the Trinity, giving a separate place to the Son of God, Who is the truly subsisting power of the Father, and a separate place to Him Who was crucified as though He were different from the Mighty One, or as though the Holy Trinity was considered passible, and the Father and the Holy Spirit suffered on the Cross along with the Son. Have done with this blasphemous and nonsensical interpolation! For we hold the words Holy God to refer to the Father, without limiting the title of divinity to Him alone, but acknowledging also as God the Son and the Holy Spirit: and the words Holy and Mighty we ascribe to the Son, without stripping the Father and the Holy Spirit of might: and the words Holy and Immortal we attribute to the Holy Spirit, without depriving the Father and the Son of immortality. For, indeed, we apply all the divine names simply and unconditionally to each of the subsistences in imitation of the divine Apostle's words. *But to us there is but one God, the Father, of Whom are all things, and we in Him: and one Lord Jesus Christ by Whom are all things, and we by Him* 1 Corinthians 8:5. And, nevertheless, we follow Gregory the Theologian when he says, But to us there is but one God, the Father, of Whom are all things, and one Lord Jesus Christ, through Whom are all things, and one Holy Spirit, in Whom are all things: for the words of Whom and through Whom and in Whom do not divide the natures (for neither the prepositions nor the order of the names could ever be changed), but they characterise the properties of one unconfused nature. And this becomes clear from the fact that they are once more gathered into one, if only one reads with care these words of the same Apostle, *Of Him and through Him and in Him are all things: to Him be the glory for ever and ever. Amen* Romans 11:36 .

For that the Trisagium refers not to the Son alone , but to the Holy Trinity, the divine and saintly Athanasius and Basil and Gregory, and all the band of the divinely-inspired Fathers bear witness: because, as a matter of fact, by the threefold holiness the Holy Seraphim suggest to us the three subsistences of the superessential Godhead. But by the one Lordship they denote the one essence and dominion of the supremely-divine Trinity. Gregory the Theologian of a truth says , Thus, then, the Holy of Holies, which is completely veiled by the Seraphim, and is glorified with three consecrations, meet together in one lordship and one divinity. This was the most beautiful and sublime philosophy of still another of our predecessors.

Ecclesiastical historians , then, say that once when the people of Constantinople were offering prayers to God to avert a threatened calamity , during Proclus' tenure of the office of Archbishop, it happened that a boy was snatched up from among the people, and was taught by angelic teachers the Thrice Holy Hymn, Thou Holy God, Holy and Mighty One, Holy and Immortal One, have mercy upon us: and when once more he was restored to earth, he told what he had learned, and all the people sang the Hymn, and so the threatened calamity was averted. And in the fourth holy and great Œcumenical Council, I mean the one at Chalcedon, we are told that it was in this form that the Hymn was sung; for the minutes of this holy assembly so record it. It is, therefore, a matter for laughter and ridicule that this Thrice Holy Hymn, taught us by the angels, and confirmed by the averting of calamity , ratified and established by so great an assembly of the holy Fathers, and sung first by the Seraphim as a declaration of the three subsistences of the Godhead, should be mangled and forsooth emended to suit the view of the stupid Fuller as though he were higher than the Seraphim. But oh! The arrogance! not to say folly! But we say it thus, though demons should rend us in pieces, Do Thou, Holy God, Holy and Mighty One, Holy and Immortal One, have mercy upon us.

Chapter 11. Concerning the Nature as viewed in Species and in Individual, and concerning the difference between Union and Incarnation: and how this is to be understood, The one Nature of God the Word Incarnate.

Nature is regarded either abstractly as a matter of pure thought (for it has no independent existence): or commonly in all subsistences of the same species as their bond of union, and is then spoken of as nature viewed in species: or universally as the same, but with the addition of accidents, in one subsistence, and is spoken of as nature viewed in the individual, this being identical with nature viewed in species. God the Word Incarnate, therefore, did not assume the nature that is regarded as an abstraction in pure thought (for this is not incarnation, but only an imposture and a figment of incarnation), nor the nature viewed in species (for He did not assume all the subsistences): but the nature viewed in the individual, which is identical with that viewed in species. For He took on Himself the elements of our compound nature, and these not as having an independent existence or as being originally an individual, and in this way assumed by Him, but as existing in His own subsistence. For the subsistence of God the Word in itself became the subsistence of the flesh, and accordingly the Word became flesh John 1:14 clearly without any change, and likewise the flesh became Word without alteration, and God became man. For the Word is God, and man is God, through having one and the same subsistence. And so it is possible to speak of the same thing as being the nature of the Word and the nature in the individual. For it signifies strictly and exclusively neither the individual, that is, the subsistence, nor the common nature of the subsistences, but the common nature as viewed and presented in one of the subsistences.

Union, then, is one thing, and incarnation is something quite different. For union signifies only the conjunction, but not at all that with which union is effected. But incarnation (which is just the same as if one said the putting on of man's nature) signifies that the conjunction is with flesh, that is to say, with man, just as the heating of iron implies its union with fire. Indeed, the blessed Cyril himself, when he is interpreting the phrase, one nature of God the Word Incarnate, says in the second epistle to Sucensus, For if we simply said 'the one nature of the Word' and then were silent, and did not add the word 'incarnate,' but, so to speak, quite excluded the dispensation , there would be some plausibility in the question they feign to ask, 'If one nature is the whole, what becomes of the perfection in humanity, or how has the essence like us come to exist.' But inasmuch as the perfection in humanity and the disclosure of the essence like us are conveyed in the word 'incarnate,' they must cease from relying on a mere straw. Here, then, he placed the nature of the Word over nature itself. For if He had received nature instead of subsistence, it would not have been absurd to have omitted the incarnate. For when we say simply one subsistence of God the Word, we do not err. In like manner, also, Leontius the Byzantine considered this phrase to refer to nature, and not to subsistence. But in the Defence which he wrote in reply to the attacks that Theodoret made on the second anathema, the blessed Cyril says this: The nature of the Word, that is, the subsistence, which is the Word itself. So that the nature of the Word means neither the subsistence alone, nor the common nature of the subsistence, but the common nature viewed as a whole in the subsistence of the Word.

It has been said, then, that the nature of the Word became flesh, that is, was united to flesh: but that the nature of the Word suffered in the flesh we have never heard up till now, though we have been taught that Christ suffered in the flesh. So that the nature of the Word does not mean the subsistence. It remains, therefore, to say that to become flesh is to be united with the flesh, while the Word having become flesh means that the very subsistence of the Word became without change the subsistence of the flesh. It has also been said that God became man, and man God. For the Word which is God became without alteration man. But that the Godhead became man, or became flesh, or put on the nature of man, this we have never heard. This, indeed, we have learned, that the Godhead was united to humanity in one of its subsistences, and it has been stated that God took on a different form or essence, to wit our own. For the name God is applicable to each of the subsistences, but we cannot use the term Godhead in reference to subsistence. For we are never told that the Godhead is the Father alone, or the Son alone, or the Holy Spirit alone. For Godhead implies nature, while Father implies subsistence, just as Humanity implies nature, and Peter subsistence. But God indicates the common element of the nature, and is applicable derivatively to each of the subsistences, just as man is. For He Who has divine nature is God, and he who has human nature is man.

Besides all this, notice that the Father and the Holy Spirit take no part at all in the incarnation of the Word except in connection with the miracles, and in respect of good will and purpose.

Chapter 12. That the holy Virgin is the Mother of God: an argument directed against the Nestorians.

Moreover we proclaim the holy Virgin to be in strict truth the Mother of God. For inasmuch as He who was born of her was true God, she who bare the true God incarnate is the true mother of God. For we hold that God was born of her, not implying that the divinity of the Word received from her the beginning of its being, but meaning that God the Word Himself, Who was begotten of the Father timelessly before the ages, and was with the Father and the Spirit without beginning and through eternity, took up His abode in these last days for the sake of our salvation in the Virgin's womb, and was without change made flesh and born of her. For the holy Virgin did not bare mere man but true God: and not mere God but God incarnate, Who did not bring down His body from Heaven, nor simply passed through the Virgin as channel, but received from her flesh of like essence to our own and subsisting in Himself. For if the body had come down from heaven and had not partaken of our nature, what would have been the use of His becoming man? For the purpose of God the Word becoming man was that the very same nature, which had sinned and fallen and become corrupted, should triumph over the deceiving tyrant and so be freed from corruption, just as the divine apostle puts it, *For since by man came death, by man came also the resurrection of the dead.* 1 Corinthians 15:21 If the first is true the second must also be true.

Although, however, he says, *The first Adam is of the earth earthy; the second Adam is Lord from Heaven* 1 Corinthians 15:47, he does not say that His body is from heaven, but emphasises the fact that He is not mere man. For, mark, he called Him both Adam and Lord, thus indicating His double nature. For Adam is, being interpreted, earth-born: and it is clear that man's nature is earth-born since he is formed from earth, but the title Lord signifies His divine essence.

And again the Apostle says: *God sent forth His only-begotten Son, made of a woman.* Galatians 4:4 He did not say made by a woman. Wherefore the divine apostle meant that the only-begotten Son of God and God is the same as He who was made man of the Virgin, and that He who was born of the Virgin is the same as the Son of God and God.

But He was born after the bodily fashion inasmuch as He became man, and did not take up His abode in a man formed beforehand, as in a prophet, but became Himself in essence and truth man, that is He caused flesh animated with the intelligent and reasonable to subsist in His own subsistence, and Himself became subsistence for it. For this is the meaning of made of a woman. For how could the very Word of God itself have been made under the law, if He did not become man of like essence with ourselves?

Hence it is with justice and truth that we call the holy Mary the Mother of God. For this name embraces the whole mystery of the dispensation. For if she who bore Him is the Mother of God, assuredly He Who was born of her is God and likewise also man. For how could God, Who was before the ages, have been born of a woman unless He had become man? For the son of man must clearly be man himself. But if He Who was born of a woman is Himself God, manifestly He Who was born of God the Father in accordance with the laws of an essence that is divine and knows no beginning, and He Who was in the last days born of the Virgin in accordance with the laws of an essence that has beginning and is subject to time, that is, an essence which is human, must be one and the same. The name in truth signifies the one subsistence and the two natures and the two generations of our Lord Jesus Christ.

But we never say that the holy Virgin is the Mother of Christ [χριστοτόκος, as opposed to θεοτόκος] because it was in order to do away with the title Mother of God, and to bring dishonour on the Mother of God, who alone is in truth worthy of honour above all creation, that the impure and abominable Judaizing Nestorius , that vessel of dishonour, invented this name for an insult. For David the king, and Aaron, the high priest, are also called *Christ* , for it is customary to make kings and priests by anointing: and besides every God-inspired man may be called *Christ,* but yet he is not by nature God: yea, the accursed Nestorius insulted Him Who was born of the Virgin by calling Him God-bearer. May it be far from us to speak of or think of Him as God-bearer only , Who is in truth God incarnate. For the Word Himself became flesh, having been in truth conceived of the Virgin, but coming forth as God with the assumed nature which, as soon as He was brought forth into being, was deified by Him, so that these three things took place simultaneously, the assumption of our nature, the coming into being, and the deification of the assumed nature by the Word. And thus it is that the holy Virgin is thought of and spoken of as the Mother of God, not only because of the nature of the

Word, but also because of the deification of man's nature, the miracles of conception and of existence being wrought together, to wit, the conception the Word, and the existence of the flesh in the Word Himself. For the very Mother of God in some marvellous manner was the means of fashioning the Framer of all things and of bestowing manhood on the God and Creator of all, Who deified the nature that He assumed, while the union preserved those things that were united just as they were united, that is to say, not only the divine nature of Christ but also His human nature, not only that which is above us but that which is of us. For He was not first made like us and only later became higher than us, but ever from His first coming into being He existed with the double nature, because He existed in the Word Himself from the beginning of the conception. Wherefore He is human in His own nature, but also, in some marvellous manner, of God and divine. Moreover He has the properties of the living flesh: for by reason of the dispensation the Word received these which are, according to the order of natural motion, truly natural.

Chapter 13. Concerning the properties of the two Natures.

Confessing, then, the same Jesus Christ, our Lord, to be perfect God and perfect man, we hold that the same has all the attributes of the Father save that of being ingenerate, and all the attributes of the first Adam, save only his sin, these attributes being body and the intelligent and rational soul; and further that He has, corresponding to the two natures, the two sets of natural qualities belonging to the two natures: two natural volitions, one divine and one human, two natural energies, one divine and one human, two natural free-wills, one divine and one human, and two kinds of wisdom and knowledge, one divine and one human. For being of like essence with God and the Father, He wills and energises freely as God, and being also of like essence with us He likewise wills and energises freely as man. For His are the miracles and His also are the passive states.

Chapter 14. Concerning the volitions and free-will of our Lord Jesus Christ.

Since, then, Christ has two natures, we hold that He has also two natural wills and two natural energies. But since His two natures have one subsistence, we hold that it is one and the same person who wills and energises naturally in both natures, of which, and in which, and also which is Christ our Lord: and moreover that He wills and energises without separation but as a united whole. For He wills and energises in either form in close communion with the other. For things that have the same essence have also the same will and energy, while things that are different in essence are different in will and energy ; and *vice versa*, things that have the same will and energy have the same essence, while things that are different in will and energy are different in essence.

Wherefore in the case of the Father and Son and Holy Spirit we recognise, from their sameness in will and energy, their sameness in nature. But in the case of the divine dispensation we recognise from their difference in will and energy the difference of the two natures, and as we perceive the difference of the two natures we confess that the wills and energies also are different. For just as the number of the natures of one and the same Christ, when considered and spoken of with piety, do not cause a division of the one Christ but merely bring out the fact that the difference between the natures is maintained even in the union, so it is with the number of wills and energies that belong essentially to His natures. (For He was endowed with the powers of willing and energising in both natures, for the sake of our salvation.) It does not introduce division: God forbid! But merely brings out the fact that the differences between them are safeguarded and preserved even in the union. For we hold that wills and energies are faculties belonging to nature, not to subsistence; I mean those faculties of will and energy by which He Who wills and energises does so. For if we allow that they belong to subsistence, we will be forced to say that the three subsistences of the Holy Trinity have different wills and different energies.

For it is to be noted that willing and the manner of willing are not the same thing. For to will is a faculty of nature, just as seeing is, for all men possess it; but the manner of willing does not depend on nature but on our judgment, just as does also the manner of seeing, whether well or ill. For all men do not will in the same way, nor do they all see in the same way. And this also we will grant in connection with energies. For the manner of willing, or seeing, or energising, is the mode of using the faculties of will and sight and energy, belonging only to him who uses them, and marking him off from others by the generally accepted difference.

Simple willing then is spoken of as volition or the faculty of will , being a rational propension and natural will; but in a particular way willing, or that which underlies volition, is the object of will , and will dependent on judgment. Further that which has innate in it the faculty of volition is spoken of as capable of willing : as for instance the divine is capable of willing, and the human in like manner. But he who exercises volition, that is to say the subsistence, for instance Peter, is spoken of as willing.

Since, then , Christ is one and His subsistence is one, He also Who wills both as God and as man is one and the same. And since He has two natures endowed with volition, inasmuch as they are rational (for whatever is rational is endowed with volition and free-will), we shall postulate two volitions or natural wills in Him. For He in His own person is capable of volition in accordance with both His natures. For He assumed that faculty of volition which belongs naturally to us. And since Christ, Who in His own person wills according to either nature, is one, we shall postulate the same object of will in His case, not as though He wills only those things which He willed naturally as God (for it is no part of Godhead to will to eat or drink and so forth), but as willing also those things which human nature requires for its support , and this without involving any opposition in judgment, but simply as the result of the individuality of the natures. For then it was that He thus willed naturally, when His divine volition so willed and permitted the flesh to suffer and do that which was proper to it.

But that volition is implanted in man by nature is manifest from this. Excluding the divine life, there are three forms of life: the vegetative, the sentient, and the intellectual. The properties of the vegetative life are the functions of nourishment, and growth, and production: that of the sentient life is impulse: and that of the rational and intellectual life is freedom of will. If, then, nourishment belongs by nature to the vegetative life and impulse to the sentient, freedom of will by nature belongs to the rational and intellectual life. But freedom of will is nothing else than volition. The Word, therefore, having become flesh, endowed with life and mind and free-will, became also endowed with volition.

Further, that which is natural is not the result of training: for no one learns how to think, or live, or hunger, or thirst, or sleep. Nor do we learn how to will: so that willing is natural.

And again: if in the case of creatures devoid of reason nature rules, while nature is ruled in man who is moved of his own free-will and volition, it follows, then, that man is by nature endowed with volition.

And again: if man has been made after the image of the blessed and super-essential Godhead, and if the divine nature is by nature endowed with free-will and volition, it follows that man, as its image, is free by nature and volitive. For the fathers defined freedom as volition.

And further: if to will is a part of the nature of every man and not present in some and absent in others, and if that which is seen to be common to all is a characteristic feature of the nature that belongs to the individuals of the class, surely, then, man is by nature endowed with volition.

And once more: if the nature receives neither more nor less, but all are equally endowed with volition and not some more than others, then by nature man is endowed with volition. So that since man is by nature endowed with volition, the Lord also must be by nature endowed with volition, not only because He is God, but also because He became man. For just as He assumed our nature, so also He has assumed naturally our will. And in this way the Fathers said that He formed our will in Himself.

If the will is not natural, it must be either hypostatic or unnatural. But if it is hypostatic, the Son must thus, forsooth, have a different will from what the Father has: for that which is hypostatic is characteristic of subsistence only. And if it is unnatural, will must be a defection from nature: for what is unnatural is destructive of what is natural.

The God and Father of all things wills either as Father or as God. Now if as Father, His will will be different from that of the Son, for the Son is not the Father. But if as God, the Son is God and likewise the Holy Spirit is God, and so volition is part of His nature, that is, it is natural.

Besides , if according to the view of the Fathers, those who have one and the same will have also one and the same essence, and if the divinity and humanity of Christ have one and the same will, then assuredly these have also one and the same essence.

And again: if according to the view of the Fathers the distinction between the natures is not seen in the single will, we must either, when we speak of the one will, cease to speak of the different natures in Christ or, when we speak of the different natures of Christ, cease to speak of the one will.

And further , the divine Gospel says, *The Lord came into the borders of Tyre and Sidon and entered into a house, and would have no man know it; but He could not be hid.* Mark 7:24 If, then, His divine will is omnipotent, but yet, though He would, He could not be hid, surely it was as man that He would and could not, and so as man He must be endowed with volition.

And once again , the Gospel tells us that, *He, having come into the place, said 'I thirst': and they gave Him some vinegar mixed with gall, and when He had tasted it He would not drink.* If, then, on the one hand it was as God that He suffered thirst and when He had tasted would not drink, surely He must be subject to passion also as God, for thirst and taste are passions. But if it was not as God but altogether as man that He was thirsty, likewise as man He must be endowed with volition.

Moreover, the blessed Paul the Apostle says, *He became obedient unto death, even the death of the cross.* Philippians 2:8 But obedience is subjection of the real will, not of the unreal will. For that which is irrational is not said to be obedient or disobedient. But the Lord having become obedient to the Father, became so not as God but as man. For as God He is not said to be obedient or disobedient. For these things are of the things that are under one's hand , as the inspired Gregorius said. Wherefore, then, Christ is endowed with volition as man.

While, however, we assert that will is natural, we hold not that it is dominated by necessity, but that it is free. For if it is rational, it must be absolutely free. For it is not only the divine and uncreated nature that is free from the bonds of necessity, but also the intellectual and created nature. And this is manifest: for God, being by nature good and being by nature the Creator and by nature God, is not all this of necessity. For who is there to introduce this necessity?

It is to be observed further , that freedom of will is used in several senses, one in connection with God, another in connection with angels, and a third in connection with men. For used in reference to God it is to be understood in a superessential manner, and in reference to angels it is to be taken in the sense that the election is concomitant with the state , and admits of the interposition of no interval of time at all: for while the angel possesses free-will by nature, he uses it without let or hindrance, having neither antipathy on the part of the body to overcome nor any assailant. Again, used in reference to men, it is to be taken in the sense that the state is considered to be anterior in time to the election. For man is free and has free-will by nature, but he has also the assault of the devil to impede him and the motion of the body: and thus through the assault and the weight of the body, election comes to be later than the state.

If, then, Adam obeyed of his own will and ate of his own will, surely in us the will is the first part to suffer. And if the will is the first to suffer, and the Word Incarnate did not assume this with the rest of our nature, it follows that we have not been freed from sin.

Moreover, if the faculty of free-will which is in nature is His work and yet He did not assume it, He either condemned His own workmanship as not good, or grudged us the comfort it brought, and so deprived us of the full benefit, and showed that He was Himself subject to passion since He was not willing or not able to work out our perfect salvation.

Moreover, one cannot speak of one compound thing made of two wills in the same way as a subsistence is a composition of two natures. Firstly because the compositions are of things in subsistence (*hypotasis*), not of things viewed in a different category, not in one proper to them : and secondly, because if we speak of composition of wills and energies, we will be obliged to speak of composition of the other natural properties, such as the uncreated and the created, the invisible and the visible, and so on. And what will be the name of the will that is compounded out of two wills? For the compound cannot be called by the name of the elements that make it up. For otherwise we should call that which is compounded of natures nature and not subsistence. And further, if we say that there is one compound will in Christ, we separate Him in will from the Father, for the Father's will is not compound. It remains, therefore, to say that the subsistence of Christ alone is compound and common, as in the case of the natures so also in that of the natural properties.

And we cannot , if we wish to be accurate, speak of Christ as having judgment (γνώμη) and preference. For judgment is a disposition with reference to the decision arrived at after investigation and deliberation concerning something unknown, that is to say, after counsel and decision. And after judgment comes preference , which chooses out and selects the one rather than the other. But the Lord being not mere man but also God, and knowing all things, had no need of inquiry, and investigation, and counsel, and decision, and by nature made whatever is good His own and whatever is bad foreign to Him. For thus says Isaiah the prophet, *Before the child shall know to prefer the evil, he shall choose the good; because before the child knows good or evil, he refuses wickedness by choosing the good.* For the word before proves that it is not with investigation and deliberation, as is the way with us, but as God and as subsisting in a divine manner in the flesh, that is to say, being united in subsistence to the flesh, and because of His very existence and all-embracing knowledge, that He is possessed of good in His own nature. For the virtues are natural qualities , and are implanted in all by nature and in equal measure, even if we do not all in equal measure employ our natural energies. By the transgression we were driven from the natural to the unnatural. But the Lord led us back from the unnatural into the natural. For this is what is the meaning of *in our image, after our likeness.* Genesis 1:26 And the discipline and trouble of this life were not designed as a means for our attaining virtue which was foreign to our nature, but to enable us to cast aside the evil that was foreign and contrary to our nature: just as on laboriously removing from steel the rust which is not natural to it but acquired through neglect, we reveal the natural brightness of the steel.

Observe further that the word judgment (γνώμη) is used in many ways and in many senses. Sometimes it signifies exhortation: as when the divine apostle says, *Now concerning virgins I have no commandment of the Lord; yet I give my judgment* 1 Corinthians 7:25: sometimes it means counsel, as when the prophet David says, *They have taken crafty counsel against Your people* : sometimes it means a decree, as when we read in Daniel, *Concerning whom* (or, *what*) *went this shameless decree forth* ? At other times it is used in the sense of belief, or opinion, or purpose, and, to put it shortly, the word judgment has twenty-eight different meanings.

Chapter 15. Concerning the energies in our Lord Jesus Christ.

We hold, further, that there are two energies in our Lord Jesus Christ. For He possesses on the one hand, as God and being of like essence with the Father, the divine energy, and, likewise, since He became man and of like essence to us, the energy proper to human nature.

But observe that energy and capacity for energy, and the product of energy, and the agent of energy, are all different. Energy is the efficient (δραστική) and essential activity of nature: the capacity for energy is the nature from which proceeds energy: the product of energy is that which is effected by energy: and the agent of energy is the person or subsistence which uses the energy. Further, sometimes energy is used in the sense of the product of energy, and the product of energy in that of energy, just as the terms creation and creature are sometimes transposed. For we say all creation, meaning creatures.

Note also that energy is an activity and is energised rather than energises; as Gregory the Theologian says in his thesis concerning the Holy Spirit : If energy exists, it must manifestly be energised and will not energise: and as soon as it has been energised, it will cease.

Life itself, it should be observed, is energy, yea, the primal energy of the living creature and so is the whole economy of the living creature, its functions of nutrition and growth, that is, the vegetative side of its nature, and the movement stirred by impulse, that is, the sentient side, and its activity of intellect and free-will. Energy, moreover, is the perfect realisation of power. If, then, we contemplate all these in Christ, surely we must also hold that He possesses human energy.

The first thought that arises in us is called energy: and it is simple energy not involving any relationship, the mind sending forth the thoughts peculiar to it in an independent and invisible way, for if it did not do so it could not justly be called mind. Again, the revelation and unfolding of thought by means of articulate speech is said to be energy. But this is no longer simple energy that involves no relationship, but it is considered in relation as being composed of thought and speech. Further, the very relation which he who does anything bears to that which is brought about is energy; and the very thing that is effected is called energy. The first belongs to the soul alone, the second to the soul making use of the body, the third to the body animated by mind, and the last is the effect. For the mind sees beforehand what is to be and then performs it thus by means of the body. And so the hegemony belongs to the soul, for it uses the body as an instrument, leading and restraining it. But the energy of the body is quite different, for the body is led and moved by the soul. And with regard to the effect, the touching and handling and, so to speak, the embrace of what is effected, belong to the body, while the figuration and formation belong to the soul. And so in connection with our Lord Jesus Christ, the power of miracles is the energy of His divinity, while the work of His hands and the willing and the saying, *I will, be thou clean* Matthew 8:3, are the energy of His humanity. And as to the effect, the breaking of the loaves John 6:11, and the fact that the leper heard the I will, belong to His humanity, while the multiplication of the loaves and the purification of the leper belong to His divinity. For through both, that is through the energy of the body and the energy of the soul, He displayed one and the same, cognate and equal divine energy. For just as we saw that His natures were united and permeate one another, and yet do not deny that they are different but even enumerate them, although we know they are inseparable, so also in connection with the wills and the energies we know their union, and we recognise their difference and enumerate them without introducing separation. For just as the flesh was deified without undergoing change in its own nature, in the same way also will and energy are deified without transgressing their own proper limits. For whether He is the one or the other, He is one and the same, and whether He wills and energises in one way or the other, that is as God or as man, He is one and the same.

We must, then, maintain that Christ has two energies in virtue of His double nature. For things that have diverse natures, have also different energies, and things that have diverse energies, have also different natures. And so conversely, things that have the same nature have also the same energy, and things that have one and the same energy have also one and the same essence , which is the view of the Fathers, who declare the divine meaning. One of these alternatives, then, must be true: either, if we hold that Christ has one energy, we must also hold that He has but one essence, or, if we are solicitous about truth, and confess that He has according to the doctrine of the Gospels and the Fathers two essences, we must also confess that He has two energies corresponding to and accompanying them. For as He is of like essence with God and the Father in divinity, He will be His equal also in energy. And as He likewise is of like essence with us in humanity He will be our equal also in energy. For the blessed Gregory, bishop of Nyssa, says , Things that have one and the same energy, have also absolutely the same power. For all energy is the effect of power. But it cannot be that uncreated and created nature have one and the same nature or power or energy. But if we should hold that Christ has but one energy, we should attribute to the divinity of the Word the passions of the intelligent spirit, viz. tear and grief and anguish.

If they should say , indeed, that the holy Fathers said in their disputation concerning the Holy Trinity, Things that have one and the same essence have also one and the same energy, and things which have different essences have also different energies, and that it is not right to transfer to the dispensation what has reference to matters of theology, we shall answer that if it has been said by the Fathers solely with reference to theology, and if the Son has not even after the incarnation the same energy as the Father, assuredly He cannot have the same essence. But to whom shall we attribute this, *My Father works hitherto and I work* John 5:17: and this, *Whatever things He sees the Father doing, these also does the Son likewise* : and this, *If you believe not Me, believe My works* : and this, *The work which I do bear witness concerning Me* : and this, *As the Father raised up the dead and quickens them, even so the Son quickens whom He will*. For all these show not only that He is of like essence to the Father even after the incarnation, but that He has also the same energy.

And again: if the providence that embraces all creation is not only of the Father and the Holy Spirit, but also of the Son even after the incarnation, assuredly since that is energy, He must have even after the incarnation the same energy as the Father.

But if we have learned from the miracles that Christ has the same essence as the Father, and since the miracles happen to be the energy of God, assuredly He must have even after the incarnation the same energy as the Father.

But, if there is one energy belonging to both His divinity and His humanity, it will be compound, and will be either a different energy from that of the Father, or the Father, too, will have a compound energy. But if the Father has a compound energy, manifestly He must also have a compound nature.

But if they should say that together with energy is also introduced personality , we shall reply that if personality is introduced along with energy, then the true converse must hold good that energy is also introduced along with personality; and there will be also three energies of the Holy Trinity just as there are three persons or subsistences, or there will be one person and one subsistence just as there is only one energy. Indeed, the holy Fathers have maintained with one voice that things that have the same essence have also the same energy.

But further, if personality is introduced along with energy, those who divine that neither one nor two energies of Christ are to be spoken of, do not maintain that either one or two persons of Christ are to be spoken of.

Take the case of the flaming sword; just as in it the natures of the fire and the steel are preserved distinct , so also are their two energies and their effects. For the energy of the steel is its cutting power, and that of the fire is its burning power, and the cut is the effect of the energy of the steel, and the burn is the effect of the energy of the fire: and these are kept quite distinct in the burnt cut, and in the cut burn, although neither does the burning take place apart from the cut after the union of the two, nor the cut apart from the burning: and we do not maintain on account of the twofold natural energy that there are two flaming swords, nor do we confuse the essential difference of the energies on account of the unity of the flaming sword. In like manner also, in the case of Christ, His divinity possesses an energy that is divine and omnipotent while His humanity has an energy such as is our own. And the effect of His human energy was His taking the child by the hand and drawing her to Himself, while that of His divine energy was the restoring of her to life. For the one is quite distinct from the other, although they are inseparable from one another in theandric energy. But if, because Christ has one subsistence, He must also have one energy, then, because He has one subsistence, He must also have one essence.

And again: if we should hold that Christ has but one energy, this must be either divine or human, or neither. But if we hold that it is divine we must maintain that He is God alone, stripped of our humanity. And if we hold that it is human, we shall be guilty of the impiety of saying that He is mere man. And if we hold that it is neither divine nor human, we must also hold that He is neither God nor man, of like essence neither to the Father nor to us. For it is as a result of the union that the identity in hypostasis arises, but yet the difference between the natures is not done away with. But since the difference between the natures is preserved, manifestly also the energies of the natures will be preserved. For no nature exists that is lacking in energy.

If Christ our Master has one energy, it must be either created or uncreated; for between these there is no energy, just as there is no nature. If, then, it is created, it will point to created nature alone, but if it is uncreated, it will betoken uncreated essence alone. For that which is natural must completely correspond with its nature: for there cannot exist a nature that is defective. But the energy that harmonises with nature does not belong to that which is external: and this is manifest because, apart from the energy that harmonises with nature, no nature can either exist or be known. For through that in which each thing manifests its energy, the absence of change confirms its own proper nature.

If Christ has one energy, it must be one and the same energy that performs both divine and human actions. But there is no existing thing which abiding in its natural state can act in opposite ways: for fire does not freeze and boil, nor does water dry up and make wet. How then could He Who is by nature God, and Who became by nature man, have both performed miracles, and endured passions with one and the same energy?

If, then, Christ assumed the human mind, that is to say, the intelligent and reasonable soul, undoubtedly He has thought, and will think forever. But thought is the energy of the mind: and so Christ, as man, is endowed with energy, and will be so forever.

Indeed, the most wise and great and holy John Chrysostom says in his interpretation of the Acts, in the second discourse , One would not err if he should call even His passion action: for in that He suffered all things, He accomplished that great and marvellous work, the overthrow of death, and all His other works.

If all energy is defined as essential movement of some nature, as those who are versed in these matters say, where does one perceive any nature that has no movement, and is completely devoid of energy, or where does one find energy that is not movement of natural power? But, as the blessed Cyril says , no one in his senses could admit that there was but one natural energy of God and His creation. It is not His human nature that raises up Lazarus from the dead, nor is it His divine power that sheds tears: for the shedding of tears is peculiar to human nature while the life is peculiar to the enhypostatic life. But yet they are common the one to the other, because of the identity in subsistence. For Christ is one, and one also is His person or subsistence, but yet He has two natures, one belonging to His humanity, and another belonging to His divinity. And the glory, indeed, which proceeded naturally from His divinity became common to both through the identity in subsistence, and again on account of His flesh that which was lowly became common to both. For He Who is the one or the other, that is God or man, is one and the same, and both what is divine and what is human belong to Himself. For while His divinity performed the miracles, they were not done apart from the flesh, and while His flesh performed its lowly offices, they were not done apart from the divinity. For His divinity was joined to the suffering flesh, yet remaining without passion, and endured the saving passions, and the holy mind was joined to the energising divinity of the Word, perceiving and knowing what was being accomplished.

And thus His divinity communicates its own glories to the body while it remains itself without part in the sufferings of the flesh. For His flesh did not suffer through His divinity in the same way that His divinity energised through the flesh. For the flesh acted as the instrument of His divinity. Although, therefore, from the first conception there was no division at all between the two forms , but the actions of either form through all the time became those of one person, nevertheless we do not in any way confuse those things that took place without separation, but recognise from the quality of its works what sort of form anything has.

Christ, then, energises according to both His natures and either nature energises in Him in communion with the other, the Word performing through the authority and power of its divinity all the actions proper to the Word, i.e. all acts of supremacy and sovereignty, and the body performing all the actions proper to the body, in obedience to the will of the Word that is united to it, and of whom it has become a distinct part. For He was not moved of Himself to the natural passions , nor again did He in that way recoil from the things of pain, and pray for release from them, or suffer what befell from without, but He was moved in conformity with His nature, the Word willing and allowing Him œconomically to suffer that, and to do the things proper to Him, that the truth might be confirmed by the works of nature.

Moreover, just as He received in His birth of a virgin superessential essence, so also He revealed His human energy in a superhuman way, walking with earthly feet on unstable water, not by turning the water into earth, but by causing it in the superabundant power of His divinity not to flow away nor yield beneath the weight of material feet. For not in a merely human way did He do human things: for He was not only man, but also God, and so even His sufferings brought life and salvation: nor yet did He energise as God, strictly after the manner of God, for He was not only God, but also man, and so it was by touch and word and such like that He worked miracles.

But if any one should say, We do not say that Christ has but one nature, in order to do away with His human energy, but we do so because human energy, in opposition to divine energy, is called passion ($\pi\acute{\alpha}\tau\theta\text{o}\varsigma$), we shall answer that, according to this reasoning, those also who hold that He has but one nature do not maintain this with a view to doing away with His human nature, but because human nature in opposition to divine nature is spoken of as passible ($\pi\alpha\theta\eta\tau\iota\varkappa\acute{\eta}$) . But God forbid that we should call the human activity passion, when we are distinguishing it from divine energy. For, to speak generally, of nothing is the existence recognised or defined by comparison or collation. If it were so, indeed, existing things would turn out to be mutually the one the cause of the other. For if the human activity is passion because the divine activity is energy, assuredly also the human nature must be wicked because the divine nature is good, and, by conversion and opposition, if the divine activity is called energy because the human activity is called passion, then also the divine nature must be good because the human nature is bad. And so all created things must be bad, and he must have spoken falsely who said, *And God saw every thing that He had made, and, behold, it was very good* Genesis 1:31 .

We, therefore, maintain that the holy Fathers gave various names to the human activity according to the underlying notion. For they called it power, and energy, and difference, and activity, and property, and quality, and passion, not in distinction from the divine activity, but power, because it is a conservative and invariable force; and energy, because it is a distinguishing mark, and reveals the absolute similarity between all things of the same class; and difference, because it distinguishes; and activity, because it makes manifest; and property, because it is constituent and belongs to that alone, and not to any other; and quality, because it gives form; and passion, because it is moved. For all things that are of God and after God suffer in respect of being moved, forasmuch as they have not in themselves motion or power. Therefore, as has been said, it is not in order to distinguish the one from the other that it has been named, but it is in accordance with the plan implanted in it in a creative manner by the Cause that framed the universe. Wherefore, also, when they spoke of it along with the divine nature they called it energy. For he who said, For either form energises close communion with the other , did something quite different from him who said, *And when He had fasted forty days, He was afterwards an hungered* Matthew 4:2: (for He allowed His nature to energise when it so willed, in the way proper to itself ,) or from those who hold there is a different energy in Him or that He has a twofold energy, or now one energy and now another. For these statements with the change in terms signify the two energies. Indeed, often the number is indicated both by change of terms and by speaking of them as divine and human. For the difference is difference in differing things, but how do things that do not exist differ?

Chapter 16. In reply to those who say If man has two natures and two energies, Christ must be held to have three natures and as many energies.

Each individual man, since he is composed of two natures, soul and body, and since these natures are unchangeable in him, could appropriately be spoken of as two natures: for he preserves even after their union you natural properties of either. For the body is not immortal, but corruptible; neither is the soul mortal, but immortal: and the body is not invisible nor the soul visible to bodily eyes: but the soul is rational and intellectual, and incorporeal, while the body is dense and visible, and irrational. But things that are opposed to one another in essence have not one nature, and, therefore, soul and body cannot have one essence.

And again: if man is a rational and mortal animal, and every definition is explanatory of the underlying natures, and the rational is not the same as the mortal according to the plan of nature, man then certainly cannot have one nature, according to the rule of his own definition.

But if man should at any time be said to have one nature, the word nature is here used instead of species, as when we say that man does not differ from man in any difference of nature. But since all men are fashioned in the same way, and are composed of soul and body, and each has two distinct natures, they are all brought under one definition. And this is not unreasonable, for the holy Athanasius spoke of all created things as having one nature forasmuch as they were all produced, expressing himself thus in his Oration against those who blasphemed the Holy Spirit: That the Holy Spirit is above all creation, and different from the nature of things produced and peculiar to divinity, we may again perceive. For whatever is seen to be common to many things, and not more in one and less in another, is called essence. Since, then, every man is composed of soul and body, accordingly we speak of man as having one nature. But we cannot speak of our Lord's subsistence as one nature: for each nature preserves, even after the union, its natural properties, nor can we find a class of Christs. For no other Christ was born both of divinity and of humanity to be at once God and man.

And again: man's unity in species is not the same thing as the unity of soul and body in essence. For man's unity in species makes clear the absolute similarity between all men, while the unity of soul and body in essence is an insult to their very existence, and reduces them to nothingness: for either the one must change into the essence of the other, or from different things something different must be produced, and so both would be changed, or if they keep to their own proper limits there must be two natures. For, as regards the nature of essence the corporeal is not the same as the incorporeal. Therefore, although holding that man has one nature, not because the essential quality of his soul and that of his body are the same, but because the individuals included under the species are exactly the same, it is not necessary for us to maintain that Christ also has one nature, for in this case there is no species embracing many subsistences.

Moreover, every compound is said to be composed of what immediately composes it. For we do not say that a house is composed of earth and water, but of bricks and timber. Otherwise, it would be necessary to speak of man as composed of at least five things, viz., the four elements and soul. And so also, in the case of our Lord Jesus Christ we do not look at the parts of the parts, but at those divisions of which He is immediately composed, viz., divinity and humanity.

And further, if by saying that man has two natures we are obliged to hold that Christ has three, you, too, by saying that man is composed of two natures must hold that Christ is composed of three natures: and it is just the same with the energies. For energy must correspond with nature: and Gregory the Theologian bears witness that man is said to have and has two natures, saying, God and man are two natures, since, indeed, soul and body also are two natures. And in his discourse Concerning Baptism he says, Since we consist of two parts, soul and body, the visible and the invisible nature, the purification is likewise twofold, that is, by water and Spirit.

Chapter 17. Concerning the deification of the nature of our Lord's flesh and of His will.

It is worthy of note that the flesh of the Lord is not said to have been deified and made equal to God and God in respect of any change or alteration, or transformation, or confusion of nature: as Gregory the Theologian says, Whereof the one deified, and the other was deified, and, to speak boldly, made equal to God: and that which anointed became man, and that which was anointed became God. For these words do not mean any change in nature, but rather the œconomical union (I mean the union in subsistence by virtue of which it was united inseparably with God the Word), and the permeation of the natures through one another, just as we saw that burning permeated the steel. For, just as we confess that God became man without change or alteration, so we consider that the flesh became God without change. For because the Word became flesh, He did not overstep the limits of His own divinity nor abandon the divine glories that belong to Him: nor, on the other hand, was the flesh, when deified, changed in its own nature or in its natural properties. For even after the union, both the natures abode unconfused and their properties unimpaired. But the flesh of the Lord received the riches of the divine energies through the purest union with the Word, that is to say, the union in subsistence, without entailing the loss of any of its natural attributes. For it is not in virtue of any energy of its own but through the Word united to it, that it manifests divine energy: for the flaming steel burns, not because it has been endowed in a physical way with burning energy, but because it has obtained this energy by its union with fire.

Wherefore the same flesh was mortal by reason of its own nature and life-giving through its union with the Word in subsistence. And we hold that it is just the same with the deification of the will ; for its natural activity was not changed but united with His divine and omnipotent will, and became the will of God, made man. And so it was that, though He wished, He could not of Himself escape Mark 7:24, because it pleased God the Word that the weakness of the human will, which was in truth in Him, should be made manifest. But He was able to cause at His will the cleansing of the leper Matthew 8:3, because of the union with the divine will.

Observe further, that the deification of the nature and the will points most expressly and most directly both to two natures and two wills. For just as the burning does not change into fire the nature of the thing that is burnt, but makes distinct both what is burnt, and what burned it, and is indicative not of one but of two natures, so also the deification does not bring about one compound nature but two, and their union in subsistence. Gregory the Theologian, indeed, says, Whereof the one deified, the other was deified , and by the words whereof, the one, the other, he assuredly indicates two natures.

Chapter 18. Further concerning volitions and free-wills: minds, too, and knowledges and wisdoms.

When we say that Christ is perfect God and perfect man, we assuredly attribute to Him all the properties natural to both the Father and mother. For He became man in order that that which was overcome might overcome. For He Who was omnipotent did not in His omnipotent authority and might lack the power to rescue man out of the hands of the tyrant. But the tyrant would have had a ground of complaint if, after He had overcome man, God should have used force against him. Wherefore God in His pity and love for man wished to reveal fallen man himself as conqueror, and became man to restore like with like.

But that man is a rational and intelligent animal, no one will deny. How, then, could He have become man if He took on Himself flesh without soul, or soul without mind? For that is not man. Again, what benefit would His becoming man have been to us if He Who suffered first was not saved, nor renewed and strengthened by the union with divinity? For that which is not assumed is not remedied. He, therefore, assumed the whole man, even the fairest part of him, which had become diseased, in order that He might bestow salvation on the whole. And, indeed, there could never exist a mind that had not wisdom and was destitute of knowledge. For if it has not energy or motion, it is utterly reduced to nothingness.

Therefore, God the Word , wishing to restore that which was in His own image, became man. But what is that which was in His own image, unless mind? So He gave up the better and assumed the worse. For mind is in the border-land between God and flesh, for it dwells indeed in fellowship with the flesh, and is, moreover, the image of God. Mind, then, mingles with mind, and mind holds a place midway between the pureness of God and the denseness of flesh. For if the Lord assumed a soul without mind, He assumed the soul of an irrational animal.

But if the Evangelist said that *the Word was made flesh* John 1:14, note that in the Holy Scripture sometimes a man is spoken of as a soul, as, for example, *with seventy-five souls came Jacob into Egypt* : and sometimes a man is spoken of as flesh, as, for example, *All flesh shall see the salvation of God.* And accordingly the Lord did not become flesh without soul or mind, but man. He says, indeed, Himself, *Why do you seek to kill Me, a Man that has told you the truth* John 8:40? He, therefore, assumed flesh animated with the spirit of reason and mind, a spirit that holds sway over the flesh but is itself under the dominion of the divinity of the Word.

So, then, He had by nature, both as God and as man, the power of will. But His human will was obedient and subordinate to His divine will, not being guided by its own inclination, but willing those things which the divine will willed. For it was with the permission of the divine will that He suffered by nature what was proper to Him. For when He prayed that He might escape the death, it was with His divine will naturally willing and permitting it that He did so pray and agonize and fear, and again when His divine will willed that His human will should choose the death, the passion became voluntary to Him. For it was not as God only, but also as man, that He voluntarily surrendered Himself to the death. And thus He bestowed on us also courage in the face of death. So, indeed, He said before His saving passion, *Father, if it be possible, let this cup pass from Me* , manifestly as though He were to drink the cup as man and not as God. It was as man, then, that He wished the cup to pass from Him: but these are the words of natural timidity. *Nevertheless,* He said, *not My will,* that is to say, not in so far as I am of a different essence from You, *but Your will be done* , that is to say, My will and Your will, in so far as I am of the same essence as Thou. Now these are the words of a brave heart. For the Spirit of the Lord, since He truly became man in His good pleasure, on first testing its natural weakness was sensible of the natural fellow-suffering involved in its separation from the body, but being strengthened by the divine will it again grew bold in the face of death. For since He was Himself wholly God although also man, and wholly man although also God, He Himself as man subjected in Himself and by Himself His human nature to God and the Father, and became obedient to the Father, thus making Himself the most excellent type and example for us.

Of His own free-will, moreover, He exercised His divine and human will. For free-will is assuredly implanted in every rational nature. For to what end would it possess reason, if it could not reason at its own free-will? For the Creator has implanted even in the unreasoning brutes natural appetite to compel them to sustain their own nature. For devoid of reason, as they are, they cannot guide their natural appetite but are guided by it. And so, as soon as the appetite for anything has sprung up, straightway arises also the impulse for action. And thus they do not win praise or happiness for pursuing virtue, nor punishment for doing evil. But the rational nature, although it does possess a natural appetite, can guide and train it by reason wherever the laws of nature are observed. For the advantage of reason consists in this, the free-will, by which we mean natural activity in a rational subject. Wherefore in pursuing virtue it wins praise and happiness, and in pursuing vice it wins punishment.

So that the soul of the Lord being moved of its own free-will willed, but willed of its free-will those things which His divine will willed it to will. For the flesh was not moved at a sign from the Word, as Moses and all the holy men were moved at a sign from heaven. But He Himself, Who was one and yet both God and man, willed according to both His divine and His human will. Wherefore it was not in inclination but rather in natural power that the two wills of the Lord differed from one another. For His divine will was without beginning and all-effecting, as having power that kept pace with it, and free from passion; while His human will had a beginning in time, and itself endured the natural and innocent passions, and was not naturally omnipotent. But yet it was omnipotent because it truly and naturally had its origin in the God-Word.

Chapter 19. Concerning the theandric energy.

When the blessed Dionysius says that Christ exhibited to us some sort of novel theandric energy , he does not do away with the natural energies by saying that one energy resulted from the union of the divine with the human energy: for in the same way we could speak of one new nature resulting from the union of the divine with the human nature. For, according to the holy Fathers, things that have one energy have also one essence. But he wished to indicate the novel and ineffable manner in which the natural energies of Christ manifest themselves, a manner befitting the ineffable manner in which the natures of Christ mutually permeate one another, and further how strange and wonderful and, in the nature of things, unknown was His life as man , and lastly the manner of the mutual interchange arising from the ineffable union. For we hold that the energies are not divided and that the natures do not energise separately, but that each conjointly in complete community with the other energises with its own proper energy. For the human part did not energise merely in a human manner, for He was not mere man; nor did the divine part energise only after the manner of God, for He was not simply God, but He was at once God and man. For just as in the case of natures we recognise both their union and their natural difference, so is it also with the natural wills and energies.

Note, therefore, that in the case of our Lord Jesus Christ, we speak sometimes of His two natures and sometimes of His one person: and the one or the other is referred to one conception. For the two natures are one Christ, and the one Christ is two natures. Wherefore it is all the same whether we say Christ energises according to either of His natures, or either nature energises in Christ in communion with the other. The divine nature, then, has communion with the flesh in its energising, because it is by the good pleasure of the divine will that the flesh is permitted to suffer and do the things proper to itself, and because the energy of the flesh is altogether saving, and this is an attribute not of human but of divine energy. On the other hand the flesh has communion with the divinity of the Word in its energising, because the divine energies are performed, so to speak, through the organ of the body, and because He Who energises at once as God and man is one and the same.

Further observe that His holy mind also performs its natural energies, thinking and knowing that it is God's mind and that it is worshipped by all creation, and remembering the times He spent on earth and all He suffered, but it has communion with the divinity of the Word in its energising and orders and governs the universe, thinking and knowing and ordering not as the mere mind of man, but as united in subsistence with God and acting as the mind of God.

This, then, the theandric energy makes plain that when God became man, that is when He became incarnate, both His human energy was divine, that is deified, and not without part in His divine energy, and His divine energy was not without part in His human energy, but either was observed in conjunction with the other. Now this manner of speaking is called a periphrasis, viz., when one embraces two things in one statement. For just as in the case of the flaming sword we speak of the cut burn as one, and the burnt cut as one, but still hold that the cut and the burn have different energies and different natures, the burn having the nature of fire and the cut the nature of steel, in the same way also when we speak of one theandric energy of Christ, we understand two distinct energies of His two natures, a divine energy belonging to His divinity, and a human energy belonging to His humanity.

Chapter 20. Concerning the natural and innocent passions.

We confess ,then, that He assumed all the natural and innocent passions of man. For He assumed the whole man and all man's attributes save sin. For that is not natural, nor is it implanted in us by the Creator, but arises voluntarily in our mode of life as the result of a further implantation by the devil, though it cannot prevail over us by force. For the natural and innocent passions are those which are not in our power, but which have entered into the life of man owing to the condemnation by reason of the transgression; such as hunger, thirst, weariness, labour, the tears, the corruption, the shrinking from death, the fear, the agony with the bloody sweat, the succour at the hands of angels because of the weakness of the nature, and other such like passions which belong by nature to every man.

All, then, He assumed that He might sanctify all. He was tried and overcame in order that He might prepare victory for us and give to nature power to overcome its antagonist, in order that nature which was overcome of old might overcome its former conqueror by the very weapons wherewith it had itself been overcome.

The wicked one , then, made his assault from without, not by thoughts prompted inwardly, just as it was with Adam. For it was not by inward thoughts, but by the serpent that Adam was assailed. But the Lord repulsed the assault and dispelled it like vapour, in order that the passions which assailed him and were overcome might be easily subdued by us, and that the new Adam should save the old.

Of a truth our natural passions were in harmony with nature and above nature in Christ. For they were stirred in Him after a natural manner when He permitted the flesh to suffer what was proper to it: but they were above nature because that which was natural did not in the Lord assume command over the will. For no compulsion is contemplated in Him but all is voluntary. For it was with His will that He hungered and thirsted and feared and died.

Chapter 21. Concerning ignorance and servitude.

He assumed, it is to be noted , the ignorant and servile nature. For it is man's nature to be the servant of God, his Creator, and he does not possess knowledge of the future. If, then, as Gregory the Theologian holds, you are to separate the realm of sight from the realm of thought, the flesh is to be spoken of as both servile and ignorant, but on account of the identity of subsistence and the inseparable union the soul of the Lord was enriched with the knowledge of the future as also with the other miraculous powers. For just as the flesh of men is not in its own nature life-giving, while the flesh of our Lord which was united in subsistence with God the Word Himself, although it was not exempt from the mortality of its nature, yet became life-giving through its union in subsistence with the Word, and we may not say that it was not and is not for ever life-giving: in like manner His human nature does not in essence possess the knowledge of the future, but the soul of the Lord through its union with God the Word Himself and its identity in subsistence was enriched, as I said, with the knowledge of the future as well as with the other miraculous powers.

Observe further that we may not speak of Him as servant. For the words servitude and mastership are not marks of nature but indicate relationship, to something, such as that of fatherhood and sonship. For these do not signify essence but relation.

It is just as we said, then, in connection with ignorance, that if you separate with subtle thoughts, that is, with fine imaginings, the created from the uncreated, the flesh is a servant, unless it has been united with God the Word.

But how can it be a servant when it is once united in subsistence? For since Christ is one, He cannot be His own servant and Lord. For these are not simple predications but relative. Whose servant, then could He be? His Father's? The Son, then, would not have all the Father's attributes, if He is the Father's servant and yet in no respect His own. Besides, how could the apostle say concerning us who were adopted by Him, *So that you are no longer a servant but a son* Galatians 4:7, if indeed He is Himself a servant? The word servant, then, is used merely as a title, though not in the strict meaning: but for our sakes He assumed the form of a servant and is called a servant among us. For although He is without passion, yet for our sake He was the servant of passion and became the minister of our salvation. Those, then, who say that He is a servant divide the one Christ into two, just as Nestorius did. But we declare Him to be Master and Lord of all creation, the one Christ, at once God and man, and all-knowing. *For in Him are all the treasures of wisdom and knowledge, the hidden treasures* Colossians 2:3 .

Chapter 22. Concerning His growth.

He is, moreover, said to grow in wisdom and age and grace Luke 2:52, increasing in age indeed and through the increase in age manifesting the wisdom that is in Him ; yea, further, making men's progress in wisdom and grace, and the fulfilment of the Father's goodwill, that is to say, men's knowledge of God and men's salvation, His own increase, and everywhere taking as His own that which is ours. But those who hold that He progressed in wisdom and grace in the sense of receiving some addition to these attributes, do not say that the union took place at the first origin of the flesh, nor yet do they give precedence to the union in subsistence, but giving heed to the foolish Nestorius they imagine some strange relative union and mere indwelling, *understanding neither what they say nor whereof they affirm.* 1 Timothy 1:1 For if in truth the flesh was united with God the Word from its first origin, or rather if it existed in Him and was identical in subsistence with Him, how was it that it was not endowed completely with all wisdom and grace? Not that it might itself participate in the grace, nor share by grace in what belonged to the Word, but rather by reason of the union in subsistence, since both what is human and what is divine belong to the one Christ, and that He Who was Himself at once God and man should pour forth like a fountain over the universe His grace and wisdom and plenitude of every blessing.

Chapter 23. Concerning His Fear.

The word fear has a double meaning. For fear is natural when the soul is unwilling to be separated from the body, on account of the natural sympathy and close relationship planted in it in the beginning by the Creator, which makes it fear and struggle against death and pray for an escape from it. It may be defined thus: natural fear is the force whereby we cling to being with shrinking. For if all things were brought by the Creator out of nothing into being, they all have by nature a longing after being and not after non-being. Moreover the inclination towards those things that support existence is a natural property of them. Hence God the Word when He became man had this longing, manifesting, on the one hand, in those things that support existence, the inclination of His nature in desiring food and drink and sleep, and having in a natural manner made proof of these things, while on the other hand displaying in those things that bring corruption His natural disinclination in voluntarily shrinking in the hour of His passion before the face of death. For although what happened did so according to the laws of nature, yet it was not, as in our case, a matter of necessity. For He willingly and spontaneously accepted that which was natural. So that fear itself and terror and agony belong to the natural and innocent passions and are not under the dominion of sin.

Again, there is a fear which arises from treachery of reasoning and want of faith, and ignorance of the hour of death, as when we are at night affected by fear at some chance noise. This is unnatural fear, and may be thus defined: unnatural fear is an unexpected shrinking. This our Lord did not assume. Hence He never felt fear except in the hour of His passion, although He often experienced a feeling of shrinking in accordance with the dispensation. For He was not ignorant of the appointed time.

But the holy Athanasius in his discourse against Apollinarius says that He did actually feel fear. Wherefore the Lord said: *Now is My soul troubled.* John 12:27 The 'now' indeed means just 'when He willed,' but yet points to what actually was. For He did not speak of what was not, as though it were present, as if the things that were said only apparently happened. For all things happened naturally and actually. And again, after some other matters, he says, In nowise does His divinity admit passion apart from a suffering body, nor yet does it manifest trouble and pain apart from a pained and troubled soul, nor does it suffer anguish and offer up prayer apart from a mind that suffered anguish and offered up prayer. For, although these occurrences were not due to any overthrow of nature, yet they took place to show forth His real being. The words these occurrences were not due to any overthrow of His nature, prove that it was not involuntarily that He endured these things.

Chapter 24. Concerning our Lord's Praying.

Prayer is an uprising of the mind to God or a petitioning of God for what is fitting. How then did it happen that our Lord offered up prayer in the case of Lazarus, and at the hour of His passion? For His holy mind was in no need either of any uprising towards God, since it had been once and for all united in subsistence with the God Word, or of any petitioning of God. For Christ is one. But it was because He appropriated to Himself our personality and took our impress on Himself, and became an ensample for us, and taught us to ask of God and strain towards Him, and guided us through His own holy mind in the way that leads up to God. For just as He endured the passion, achieving for our sakes a triumph over it, so also He offered up prayer, guiding us, as I said, in the way that leads up to God, and fulfilling all righteousness Matthew 3:15 on our behalf, as He said to John, and reconciling His Father to us, and honouring Him as the beginning and cause, and proving that He is no enemy of God. For when He said in connection with Lazarus, *Father, I thank You that You have heard Me. And I know that You hear Me always, but because of the people which stand by I said it, that they may believe that You have sent Me* John 11:42, is it not most manifest to all that He said this in honour of His Father as the cause even of Himself, and to show that He was no enemy of God ?

Again, when he said, *Father, if it be possible, let this cup pass from Me: yet, not as I will but as You will* Matthew 26:39, is it not clear to all that He said this as a lesson to us to ask help in our trials only from God, and to prefer God's will to our own, and as a proof that He did actually appropriate to Himself the attributes of our nature, and that He did in truth possess two wills, natural, indeed, and corresponding with His natures but yet in no wise opposed to one another? Father implies that He is of the same essence, but if it be possible does not mean that He was in ignorance (for what is impossible to God?), but serves to teach us to prefer God's will to our own. For that alone is impossible which is against God's will and permission. But not as I will but as You will, for inasmuch as He is God, He is identical with the Father, while inasmuch as He is man, He manifests the natural will of mankind. For it is this that naturally seeks escape from death.

Further, these words, *My God, My God, why have You forsaken Me* Matthew 27:46? He said as making our personality His own. For neither would God be regarded with us as His Father, unless one were to discriminate with subtle imaginings of the mind between that which is seen and that which is thought, nor was He ever forsaken by His divinity: nay, it was we who were forsaken and disregarded. So that it was as appropriating our personality that He offered these prayers.

Chapter 25. Concerning the Appropriation.

It is to be observed that there are two appropriations : one that is natural and essential, and one that is personal and relative. The natural and essential one is that by which our Lord in His love for man took on Himself our nature and all our natural attributes, becoming in nature and truth man, and making trial of that which is natural: but the personal and relative appropriation is when any one assumes the person of another relatively, for instance, out of pity or love, and in his place utters words concerning him that have no connection with himself. And it was in this way that our Lord appropriated both our curse and our desertion, and such other things as are not natural: not that He Himself was or became such, but that He took upon Himself our personality and ranked Himself as one of us. Such is the meaning in which this phrase is to be taken: *Being made a curse for our sakes* Galatians 3:15 .

Chapter 26. Concerning the Passion of our Lord's body, and the Impassibility of His divinity.

The Word of God then itself endured all in the flesh, while His divine nature which alone was passionless remained void of passion. For since the one Christ, Who is a compound of divinity and humanity, and exists in divinity and humanity, truly suffered, that part which is capable of passion suffered as it was natural it should, but that part which was void of passion did not share in the suffering. For the soul, indeed, since it is capable of passion shares in the pain and suffering of a bodily cut, though it is not cut itself but only the body: but the divine part which is void of passion does not share in the suffering of the body.

Observe, further , that we say that God suffered in the flesh, but never that His divinity suffered in the flesh, or that God suffered through the flesh. For if, when the sun is shining upon a tree, the axe should cleave the tree, and, nevertheless, the sun remains uncleft and void of passion, much more will the passionless divinity of the Word, united in subsistence to the flesh, remain void of passion when the body undergoes passion. And should any one pour water over flaming steel, it is that which naturally suffers by the water, I mean, the fire, that is quenched, but the steel remains untouched (for it is not the nature of steel to be destroyed by water): much more, then, when the flesh suffered did His only passionless divinity escape all passion although abiding inseparable from it. For one must not take the examples too absolutely and strictly: indeed, in the examples, one must consider both what is like and what is unlike, otherwise it would not be an example. For, if they were like in all respects they would be identities, and not examples, and all the more so in dealing with divine matters. For one cannot find an example that is like in all respects whether we are dealing with theology or the dispensation.

Chapter 27. Concerning the fact that the divinity of the Word remained inseparable from the soul and the body, even at our Lord's death, and that His subsistence continued one.

Since our Lord Jesus Christ was without sin (*for He committed no sin, He Who took away the sin of the world, nor was there any deceit found in His mouth*) He was not subject to death, since death came into the world through sin. Romans 5:12 He dies, therefore, because He took on Himself death on our behalf, and He makes Himself an offering to the Father for our sakes. For we had sinned against Him, and it was meet that He should receive the ransom for us, and that we should thus be delivered from the condemnation. God forbid that the blood of the Lord should have been offered to the tyrant. Wherefore death approaches, and swallowing up the body as a bait is transfixed on the hook of divinity, and after tasting of a sinless and life-giving body, perishes, and brings up again all whom of old he swallowed up. For just as darkness disappears on the introduction of light, so is death repulsed before the assault of life, and brings life to all, but death to the destroyer.

Wherefore, although He died as man and His Holy Spirit was severed from His immaculate body, yet His divinity remained inseparable from both, I mean, from His soul and His body, and so even thus His one hypostasis was not divided into two hypostases. For body and soul received simultaneously in the beginning their being in the subsistence of the Word, and although they were severed from one another by death, yet they continued, each of them, having the one subsistence of the Word. So that the one subsistence of the Word is alike the subsistence of the Word, and of soul and body. For at no time had either soul or body a separate subsistence of their own, different from that of the Word, and the subsistence of the Word is for ever one, and at no time two. So that the subsistence of Christ is always one. For, although the soul was separated from the body topically, yet hypostatically they were united through the Word.

Chapter 28. Concerning Corruption and Destruction.

The word corruption has two meanings. For it signifies all the human sufferings, such as hunger, thirst, weariness, the piercing with nails, death, that is, the separation of soul and body, and so forth. In this sense we say that our Lord's body was subject to corruption. For He voluntarily accepted all these things. But corruption means also the complete resolution of the body into its constituent elements, and its utter disappearance, which is spoken of by many preferably as destruction. The body of our Lord did not experience this form of corruption, as the prophet David says, *For You will not leave my soul in hell, neither will You allow Your holy one to see corruption.*

Wherefore to say, with that foolish Julianus and Gaïanus, that our Lord's body was incorruptible, in the first sense of the word, before His resurrection is impious. For if it were incorruptible it was not really, but only apparently, of the same essence as ours, and what the Gospel tells us happened, viz. the hunger, the thirst, the nails, the wound in His side, the death, did not actually occur. But if they only apparently happened, then the mystery of the dispensation is an imposture and a sham, and He became man only in appearance, and not in actual fact, and we are saved only in appearance, and not in actual fact. But God forbid, and may those who so say have no part in the salvation. But we have obtained and shall obtain the true salvation. But in the second meaning of the word corruption, we confess that our Lord's body is incorruptible, that is, indestructible, for such is the tradition of the inspired Fathers. Indeed, after the resurrection of our Saviour from the dead, we say that our Lord's body is incorruptible even in the first sense of the word. For our Lord by His own body bestowed the gifts both of resurrection and of subsequent incorruption even on our own body, He Himself having become to us the firstfruits both of resurrection and incorruption, and of passionlessness. 1 Corinthians 15:20 For as the divine Apostle says, *This corruptible must put on incorruption.*

Chapter 29. Concerning the Descent to Hades.

The soul when it was deified descended into Hades, in order that, just as the Sun of Righteousness Malachi 4:2 rose for those upon the earth, so likewise He might bring light to those who sit under the earth in darkness and shadow of death Isaiah 9:2: in order that just as He brought the message of peace to those upon the earth, and of release to the prisoners, and of sight to the blind , and became to those who believed the Author of everlasting salvation and to those who did not believe a reproach of their unbelief 1 Peter 3:19, so He might become the same to those in Hades : *That every knee should bow to Him, of things in heaven, and things in earth and things under the earth.* Philippians 2:10 And thus after He had freed those who had been bound for ages, straightway He rose again from the dead, showing us the way of resurrection.

BOOK IV

Chapter 1. Concerning what followed the Resurrection.

After Christ was risen from the dead He laid aside all His passions, I mean His corruption or hunger or thirst or sleep or weariness or such like. For, although He did taste food after the resurrection Luke 24:43, yet He did not do so because it was a law of His nature (for He felt no hunger), but in the way of economy, in order that He might convince us of the reality of the resurrection, and that it was one and the same flesh which suffered and rose again. But He laid aside none of the divisions of His nature, neither body nor spirit, but possesses both the body and the soul intelligent and reasonable, volitional and energetic, and in this wise He sits at the right hand of the Father, using His will both as God and as man in behalf of our salvation, energising in His divine capacity to provide for and maintain and govern all things, and remembering in His human capacity the time He spent on earth, while all the time He both sees and knows that He is adored by all rational creation. For His Holy Spirit knows that He is one in substance with God the Word, and shares as Spirit of God and not simply as Spirit the worship accorded to Him. Moreover, His ascent from earth to heaven, and again, His descent from heaven to earth, are manifestations of the energies of His circumscribed body. *For He shall so come again to you, says he, in like manner as you have seen Him go into Heaven* Acts 1:11 .

Chapter 2. Concerning the sitting at the right hand of the Father.

We hold, moreover, that Christ sits in the body at the right hand of God the Father, but we do not hold that the right hand of the Father is actual place. For how could He that is uncircumscribed have a right hand limited by place? Right hands and left hands belong to what is circumscribed. But we understand the right hand of the Father to be the glory and honour of the Godhead in which the Son of God, who existed as God before the ages, and is of like essence to the Father, and in the end became flesh, has a seat in the body, His flesh sharing in the glory. For He along with His flesh is adored with one adoration by all creation.

Chapter 3. In reply to those who say If Christ has two natures, either you do service to the creature in worshipping created nature, or you say that there is one nature to be worshipped, and another not to be worshipped.

Along with the Father and the Holy Spirit we worship the Son of God, Who was incorporeal before He took on humanity, and now in His own person is incarnate and has become man though still being also God. His flesh, then, in its own nature , if one were to make subtle mental distinctions between what is seen and what is thought, is not deserving of worship since it is created. But as it is united with God the Word, it is worshipped on account of Him and in Him. For just as the king deserves homage alike when un-robed and when robed, and just as the purple robe, considered simply as a purple robe, is trampled upon and tossed about, but after becoming the royal dress receives all honour and glory, and whoever dishonours it is generally condemned to death: and again, just as wood in itself is not of such a nature that it cannot be touched, but becomes so when fire is applied to it, and it becomes charcoal, and yet this is not because of its own nature, but because of the fire united to it, and the nature of the wood is not such as cannot be touched, but rather the charcoal or burning wood: so also the flesh, in its own nature, is not to be worshipped, but is worshipped in the incarnate God Word, not because of itself, but because of its union in subsistence with God the Word. And we do not say that we worship mere flesh, but God's flesh, that is, God incarnate.

Chapter 4. Why it was the Son of God, and not the Father or the Spirit, that became man: and what having became man He achieved.

The Father is Father and not Son : the Son is Son and not Father: the Holy Spirit is Spirit and not Father or Son. For the individuality is unchangeable. How, indeed, could individuality continue to exist at all if it were ever changing and altering? Wherefore the Son of God became Son of Man in order that His individuality might endure. For since He was the Son of God, He became Son of Man, being made flesh of the holy Virgin and not losing the individuality of Sonship.

Further, the Son of God became man, in order that He might again bestow on man that favour for the sake of which He created him. For He created him after His own image, endowed with intellect and free-will, and after His own likeness, that is to say, perfect in all virtue so far as it is possible for man's nature to attain perfection. For the following properties are, so to speak, marks of the divine nature: viz. absence of care and distraction and guile, goodness, wisdom, justice, freedom from all vice. So then, after He had placed man in communion with Himself (for having made him for incorruption Wisdom 2:23, He led him up through communion with Himself to incorruption), and when moreover, through the transgression of the command we had confused and obliterated the marks of the divine image, and had become evil, we were stripped of our communion with God (for what communion has light with darkness 2 Corinthians 6:14?): and having been shut out from life we became subject to the corruption of death: yea, since He gave us to share in the better part, and we did not keep it secure, He shares in the inferior part, I mean our own nature, in order that through Himself and in Himself He might renew that which was made after His image and likeness, and might teach us, too, the conduct of a virtuous life, making through Himself the way there easy for us, and might by the communication of life deliver us from corruption, becoming Himself the firstfruits of our resurrection, and might renovate the useless and worn vessel calling us to the knowledge of God that He might redeem us from the tyranny of the devil, and might strengthen and teach us how to overthrow the tyrant through patience and humility.

The worship of demons then has ceased: creation has been sanctified by the divine blood: altars and temples of idols have been overthrown, the knowledge of God has been implanted in men's minds, the co-essential Trinity, the uncreate divinity, one true God, Creator and Lord of all receives men's service: virtues are cultivated, the hope of resurrection has been granted through the resurrection of Christ, the demons shudder at those men who of old were under their subjection. And the marvel, indeed, is that all this has been successfully brought about through His cross and passion and death. Throughout all the earth the Gospel of the knowledge of God has been preached; no wars or weapons or armies being used to rout the enemy, but only a few, naked, poor, illiterate, persecuted and tormented men, who with their lives in their hands, preached Him Who was crucified in the flesh and died, and who became victors over the wise and powerful. For the omnipotent power of the Cross accompanied them. Death itself, which once was man's chiefest terror, has been overthrown, and now that which was once the object of hate and loathing is preferred to life. These are the achievements of Christ's presence: these are the tokens of His power. For it was not one people that He saved, as when through Moses He divided the sea and delivered Israel out of Egypt and the bondage of Pharaoh Exodus 14:16; nay, rather He rescued all mankind from the corruption of death and the bitter tyranny of sin: not leading them by force to virtue, not overwhelming them with earth or burning them with fire, or ordering the sinners to be stoned, but persuading men by gentleness and long-suffering to choose virtue and vie with one another, and find pleasure in the struggle to attain it. For, formerly, it was sinners who were persecuted, and yet they clung all the closer to sin, and sin was looked upon by them as their God: but now for the sake of piety and virtue men choose persecutions and crucifixions and death.

Hail! O Christ, the Word and Wisdom and Power of God, and God omnipotent! What can we helpless ones give You in return for all these good gifts? For all are Yours, and Thou ask naught from us save our salvation, You Who Yourself art the Giver of this, and yet art grateful to those who receive it, through Your unspeakable goodness. Thanks be to You Who gave us life, and granted us the grace of a happy life, and restored us to that, when we had gone astray, through Your unspeakable condescension.

Chapter 5. In reply to those who ask if Christ's subsistence is create or uncreate.

The subsistence of God the Word before the Incarnation was simple and uncompound, and incorporeal and uncreate: but after it became flesh, it became also the subsistence of the flesh, and became compounded of divinity which it always possessed, and of flesh which it had assumed: and it bears the properties of the two natures, being made known in two natures: so that the one same subsistence is both uncreate in divinity and create in humanity, visible and invisible. For otherwise we are compelled either to divide the one Christ and speak of two subsistences, or to deny the distinction between the natures and thus introduce change and confusion.

Chapter 6. Concerning the question, when Christ was called.

The mind was not united with God the Word, as some falsely assert , before the Incarnation by the Virgin and from that time called Christ. That is the absurd nonsense of Origen who lays down the doctrine of the priority of the existence of souls. But we hold that the Son and Word of God became Christ after He had dwelt in the womb of His holy ever-virgin Mother, and became flesh without change, and that the flesh was anointed with divinity. For this is the anointing of humanity, as Gregory the Theologian says. And here are the words of the most holy Cyril of Alexandria which he wrote to the Emperor Theodosius : For I indeed hold that one ought to give the name Jesus Christ neither to the Word that is of God if He is without humanity, nor yet to the temple born of woman if it is not united with the Word. For the Word that is of God is understood to be Christ when united with humanity in ineffable manner in the union of the œconomy. And again, he writes to the Empresses thus : Some hold that the name 'Christ' is rightly given to the Word that is begotten of God the Father, to Him alone, and regarded separately by Himself. But we have not been taught so to think and speak. For when the Word became flesh, then it was, we say, that He was called Christ Jesus. For since He was anointed with the oil of gladness, that is the Spirit, by Him Who is God and Father, He is for this reason called Christ. But that the anointing was an act that concerned Him as man could be doubted by no one who is accustomed to think rightly. Moreover, the celebrated Athanasius says this in his discourse Concerning the Saving Manifestation: The God Who was before the sojourn in the flesh was not man, but God in God, being invisible and without passion, but when He became man, He received in addition the name of Christ because of the flesh, since, indeed, passion and death follow in the train of this name.

And although the holy Scripture says, *Therefore God, your God, has anointed you with the oil of gladness* , it is to be observed that the holy Scripture often uses the past tense instead of the future, as for example here: *Thereafter He was seen upon the earth and dwelt among men.* Baruch 3:38 For as yet God was not seen nor did He dwell among men when this was said. And here again: *By the rivers of Babylon, there we sat down; yea wept.* For as yet these things had not come to pass.

Chapter 7. In answer to those who enquire whether the holy Mother of God bore two natures, and whether two natures hung upon the Cross.

ἀγένητον and γενητόν, written with one 'ν' and meaning uncreated and created, refer to nature: but ἀγέννητον and γεννητόν, that is to say, unbegotten and begotten, as the double 'ν' indicates, refer not to nature but to subsistence. The divine nature then is ἀγένητος, that is to say, uncreate, but all things that come after the divine nature are γένητα, that is, created. In the divine and uncreated nature, therefore, the property of being ἀγέννητον or unbegotten is contemplated in the Father (for He was not begotten), that of being γέννητον or begotten in the Son (for He has been eternally begotten of the Father), and that of procession in the Holy Spirit. Moreover of each species of living creatures, the first members were ἀγέννητα but not ἀγένητα: for they were brought into being by their Maker, but were not the offspring of creatures like themselves. For γένεσις is creation, while γέννησις or begetting is in the case of God the origin of a co-essential Son arising from the Father alone, and in the case of bodies, the origin of a co-essential subsistence arising from the contact of male and female. And thus we perceive that begetting refers not to nature but to subsistence. For if it did refer to nature, τὸ γέννητον and το ἀγέννητον, i.e. the properties of being begotten and unbegotten, could not be contemplated in one and the same nature. Accordingly the holy Mother of God bore a subsistence revealed in two natures; being begotten on the one hand, by reason of its divinity, of the Father timelessly, and, at last, on the other hand, being incarnated of her in time and born in the flesh.

But if our interrogators should hint that He Who is begotten of the holy Mother of God is two natures, we reply, Yea! He is two natures: for He is in His own person God and man. And the same is to be said concerning the crucifixion and resurrection and ascension. For these refer not to nature but to subsistence. Christ then, since He is in two natures, suffered and was crucified in the nature that was subject to passion. For it was in the flesh and not in His divinity that He hung upon the Cross. Otherwise, let them answer us, when we ask if two natures died. No, we shall say. And so two natures were not crucified but Christ was begotten, that is to say, the divine Word having become man was begotten in the flesh, was crucified in the flesh, suffered in the flesh, while His divinity continued to be impassible.

Chapter 8. How the Only-begotten Son of God is called first-born.

He who is first begotten is called first-born , whether he is only-begotten or the first of a number of brothers. If then the Son of God was called first-born, but was not called Only-begotten, we could imagine that He was the first-born of creatures, as being a creature. But since He is called both first-born and Only-begotten, both senses must be preserved in His case. We say that He is first-born of all creation Colossians 1:15 since both He Himself is of God and creation is of God, but as He Himself is born alone and timelessly of the essence of God the Father, He may with reason be called Only-begotten Son, first-born and not first-created. For the creation was not brought into being out of the essence of the Father, but by His will out of nothing. And He is called First-born among many brethren Romans 8:29, for although being Only-begotten, He was also born of a mother. Since, indeed, He participated just as we ourselves do in blood and flesh and became man, while we too through Him became sons of God, being adopted through the baptism, He Who is by nature Son of God became first-born among us who were made by adoption and grace sons of God, and stand to Him in the relation of brothers. Wherefore He said, *I ascend unto My Father and your Father.* John 20:17 He did not say our Father, but My Father, clearly in the sense of Father by nature, and your Father, in the sense of Father by grace. And My God and your God. He did not say our God, but My God: and if you distinguish with subtle thought that which is seen from that which is thought, also your God, as Maker and Lord.

Chapter 9. Concerning Faith and Baptism.

We confess one baptism for the remission of sins and for life eternal. For baptism declares the Lord's death. We are indeed buried with the Lord through baptism Colossians 2:12, as says the divine Apostle. So then, as our Lord died once for all, we also must be baptized once for all, and baptized according to the Word of the Lord, *In the Name of the Father, and of the Son, and of the Holy Spirit* Matthew 28:19, being taught the confession in Father, Son, and Holy Spirit. Those , then, who, after having been baptized into Father, Son, and Holy Spirit, and having been taught that there is one divine nature in three subsistences, are rebaptized, these, as the divine Apostle says, crucify the Christ afresh. *For it is impossible, he says, for those who were once enlightened, etc., to renew them again unto repentance: seeing they crucify to themselves the Christ afresh, and put Him to an open shame.* Hebrews 6:4 But those who were not baptized into the Holy Trinity, these must be baptized again. For although the divine Apostle says: *Into Christ and into His death were we baptized* Romans 6:3, he does not mean that the invocation of baptism must be in these words, but that baptism is an image of the death of Christ. For by the three immersions , baptism signifies the three days of our Lord's entombment. The baptism then into Christ means that believers are baptized into Him. We could not believe in Christ if we were not taught confession in Father, Son, and Holy Spirit. For

Christ is the Son of the Living God Matthew 16:16, Whom the Father anointed with the Holy Spirit Acts 10:38: in the words of the divine David, *Therefore God, your God, has anointed you with the oil of gladness above your fellows.* And Isaiah also speaking in the person of the Lord says, *The Spirit of the Lord is upon me because He has anointed me.* Isaiah 61:1 Christ, however, taught His own disciples the invocation and said, *Baptizing them in the Name of the Father, and of the Son, and of the Holy Spirit.* Matthew 28:19 For since Christ made us for incorruption , and we transgressed His saving command, He condemned us to the corruption of death in order that that which is evil should not be immortal, and when in His compassion He stooped to His servants and became like us, He redeemed us from corruption through His own passion. He caused the fountain of remission to well forth for us out of His holy and immaculate side John 19:34, water for our regeneration, and the washing away of sin and corruption; and blood to drink as the hostage of life eternal. And He laid on us the command to be born again of water and of the Spirit , through prayer and invocation, the Holy Spirit drawing near unto the water. For since man's nature is twofold, consisting of soul and body, He bestowed on us a twofold purification, of water and of the Spirit: the Spirit renewing that part in us which is after His image and likeness, and the water by the grace of the Spirit cleansing the body from sin and delivering it from corruption, the water indeed expressing the image of death, but the Spirit affording the earnest of life.

For from the beginning *the Spirit of God moved upon the face of the waters* Genesis 1:2, and anew the Scripture witnesses that water has the power of purification. Leviticus 15:10 In the time of Noah God washed away the sin of the world by water. Genesis 6:17 By water every impure person is purified , according to the law, even the very garments being washed with water. Elias showed forth the grace of the Spirit mingled with the water when he burned the holocaust by pouring on water. And almost everything is purified by water according to the law: for the things of sight are symbols of the things of thought. The regeneration, however, takes place in the spirit: for faith has the power of making us sons (of God), creatures as we are, by the Spirit, and of leading us into our original blessedness.

The remission of sins, therefore, is granted alike to all through baptism: but the grace of the Spirit is proportional to the faith and previous purification. Now, indeed, we receive the firstfruits of the Holy Spirit through baptism, and the second birth is for us the beginning and seal and security and illumination of another life.

It behooves us, then, with all our strength to steadfastly keep ourselves pure from filthy works, that we may not, like the dog returning to his vomit 2 Peter 2:22, make ourselves again the slaves of sin. For faith apart from works is dead, and so likewise are works apart from faith. James 2:26 For the true faith is attested by works.

Now we are baptized into the Holy Trinity because those things which are baptized have need of the Holy Trinity for their maintenance and continuance, and the three subsistences cannot be otherwise than present, the one with the other. For the Holy Trinity is indivisible.

The first baptism was that of the flood for the eradication of sin. The second Genesis 7:17 was through the sea and the cloud: for the cloud is the symbol of the Spirit and the sea of the water. 1 Corinthians 10:1 The third baptism was that of the Law: for every impure person washed himself with water, and even washed his garments, and so entered into the camp. Leviticus 14:8 The fourth was that of John , being preliminary and leading those who were baptized to repentance, that they might believe in Christ: *I, indeed*, he said, *baptize you with water; but He that comes after me, He will baptize you in the Holy Spirit and in fire*. Matthew 3:11 Thus John's purification with water was preliminary to receiving the Spirit. The fifth was the baptism of our Lord, whereby He Himself was baptized. Now He is baptized not as Himself requiring purification but as making my purification His own, that He may break the heads of the dragons on the water, that He may wash away sin and bury all the old Adam in water, that He may sanctify the Baptist, that He may fulfil the Law, that He may reveal the mystery of the Trinity, that He may become the type and ensample to us of baptism. But we, too, are baptized in the perfect baptism of our Lord, the baptism by water and the Spirit. Moreover, Christ is said to baptize with fire: because in the form of flaming tongues He poured forth on His holy disciples the grace of the Spirit: as the Lord Himself says, *John truly baptized with water: but you shall be baptized with the Holy Spirit and with fire, not many days hence:* Acts 1:5 or else it is because of the baptism of future fire wherewith we are to be chastized. The sixth is that by repentance and tears, which baptism is truly grievous. The seventh is baptism by blood and martyrdom, which baptism Christ Himself underwent in our behalf, Luke 12:50 He Who was too august and blessed to be defiled with any later stains. The eighth is the last, which is not saving, but which destroys evil: for evil and sin no longer have sway: yet it punishes without end.

Further, the Holy Spirit descended in bodily form as a dove, indicating the firstfruits of our baptism and honouring the body: since even this, that is the body, was God by the deification; and besides the dove was wont formerly to announce the cessation of the flood. But to the holy Apostles He came down in the form of fire: for He is God, and *God is a consuming fire*. Deuteronomy 4:24

Olive oil is employed in baptism as a significant of our anointing, and as making us anointed, and as announcing to us through the Holy Spirit God's pity: for it was the fruit of the olive that the dove brought to those who were saved from the flood. Genesis 8:11

John was baptized, putting his hand upon the divine head of his Master, and with his own blood.

It does not behoove us to delay baptism when the faith of those coming forward is testified to by their works. For he that comes forward deceitfully to baptism will receive condemnation rather than benefit.

Chapter 10. Concerning Faith.

Moreover, faith is twofold. For *faith comes by hearing*. Romans 10:17 For by hearing the divine Scriptures we believe in the teaching of the Holy Spirit. The same is perfected by all the things enjoined by Christ, believing in work, cultivating piety, and doing the commands of Him Who restored us. For he that believes not according to the tradition of the Catholic Church, or who has intercourse with the devil through strange works, is an unbeliever.

But again, *faith is the substance of things hoped for, the evidence of things not seen* Hebrews 11:1, or undoubting and unambiguous hope alike of what God has promised us and of the good issue of our prayers. The first, therefore, belongs to our will, while the second is of the gifts of the Spirit.

Further, observe that by baptism we cut off all the covering which we have worn since birth, that is to say, sin, and become spiritual Israelites and God's people.

Chapter 11. Concerning the Cross and here further concerning Faith.

The word ' *Cross' is foolishness to those that perish, but to us who are saved it is the power of God.* 1 Corinthians 1:23 For *he that is spiritual judges all things, but the natural man receives not the things of the Spirit.* For it is foolishness to those who do not receive in faith and who do not consider God's goodness and omnipotence, but search out divine things with human and natural reasonings. For all the things that are of God are above nature and reason and conception. For should any one consider how and for what purpose God brought all things out of nothing and into being, and aim at arriving at that by natural reasonings, he fails to comprehend it. For knowledge of this kind belongs to spirits and demons. But if any one, under the guidance of faith, should consider the divine goodness and omnipotence and truth and wisdom and justice, he will find all things smooth and even, and the way straight. *But without faith it is impossible to be saved.* Hebrews 11:6 For it is by faith that all things, both human and spiritual, are sustained. For without faith neither does the farmer cut his furrow, nor does the merchant commit his life to the raging waves of the sea on a small piece of wood, nor are marriages contracted nor any other step in life taken. By faith we consider that all things were brought out of nothing into being by God's power. And we direct all things, both divine and human, by faith. Further, faith is assent free from all meddlesome inquisitiveness.

Every action, therefore, and performance of miracles by Christ are most great and divine and marvellous: but the most marvellous of all is His precious Cross. For no other thing has subdued death, expiated the sin of the first parent , despoiled Hades, bestowed the resurrection, granted the power to us of contemning the present and even death itself, prepared the return to our former blessedness, opened the gates of Paradise , given our nature a seat at the right hand of God, and made us the children and heirs of God , save the Cross of our Lord Jesus Christ. For by the Cross all things have been made right. *So many of us, the apostle says, as were baptized into Christ, were baptized into His death* Romans 6:3, and *as many of you as have been baptized into Christ, have put on Christ.* Galatians 3:27 Further *Christ is the power of God and the wisdom of God.* 1 Corinthians 1:24 Lo! The death of Christ, that is, the Cross, clothed us with the enhypostatic wisdom and power of God. And the power of God is the Word of the Cross, either because God's might, that is, the victory over death, has been revealed to us by it, or because, just as the four extremities of the Cross are held fast and bound together by the bolt in the middle, so also by God's power the height and the depth, the length and the breadth, that is, every creature visible and invisible, is maintained.

This was given to us as a sign on our forehead, just as the circumcision was given to Israel: for by it we believers are separated and distinguished from unbelievers. This is the shield and weapon against, and trophy over, the devil. *This is the seal that the destroyer may not touch you* Exodus 12:23, as says the Scripture. This is the resurrection of those lying in death, the support of the standing, the staff of the weak, the rod of the flock, the safe conduct of the earnest, the perfection of those that press forwards, the salvation of soul and body, the aversion of all things evil, the patron of all things good, the taking away of sin, the plant of resurrection, the tree of eternal life.

So, then, this same truly precious and august tree , on which Christ has offered Himself as a sacrifice for our sakes, is to be worshipped as sanctified by contact with His holy body and blood; likewise the nails, the spear, the clothes, His sacred tabernacles which are the manger, the cave, Golgotha, which brings salvation , the tomb which gives life, Sion, the chief stronghold of the churches and the like, are to be worshipped. In the words of David, the father of God , *We shall go into His tabernacles, we shall worship at the place where*

His feet stood. And that it is the Cross that is meant is made clear by what follows, *Arise, O Lord, into Your Rest.* For the resurrection comes after the Cross. For if of those things which we love, house and couch and garment, are to be longed after, how much the rather should we long after that which belonged to God, our Saviour , by means of which we are in truth saved.

Moreover we worship even the image of the precious and life-giving Cross, although made of another tree, not honouring the tree (God forbid) but the image as a symbol of Christ. For He said to His disciples, admonishing them, *Then shall appear the sign of the Son of Man in Heaven* Matthew 24:30, meaning the Cross. And so also the angel of the resurrection said to the woman, *You seek Jesus of Nazareth which was crucified.* Mark 16:6 And the Apostle said, *We preach Christ crucified.* 1 Corinthians 1:23 For there are many Christs and many Jesuses, but one crucified. He does not say speared but crucified. It behooves us, then, to worship the sign of Christ. For wherever the sign may be, there also will He be. But it does not behoove us to worship the material of which the image of the Cross is composed, even though it be gold or precious stones, after it is destroyed, if that should happen. Everything, therefore, that is dedicated to God we worship, conferring the adoration on Him.

The tree of life which was planted by God in Paradise pre-figured this precious Cross. For since death was by a tree, it was fitting that life and resurrection should be bestowed by a tree. Jacob, when He worshipped the top of Joseph's staff, was the first to image the Cross, and when he blessed his sons with crossed hands Hebrews 11:21 he made most clearly the sign of the cross. Likewise also did Moses' rod, when it smote the sea in the figure of the cross and saved Israel, while it overwhelmed Pharaoh in the depths; likewise also the hands stretched out crosswise and routing Amalek; and the bitter water made sweet by a tree, and the rock rent and pouring forth streams of water Numbers xx, and the rod that meant for Aaron the dignity of the high priesthood Exodus iv: and the serpent lifted in triumph on a tree as though it were dead , the tree bringing salvation to those who in faith saw their enemy dead, just as Christ was nailed to the tree in the flesh of sin which yet knew no sin. The mighty Moses cried , *You will see your life hanging on the tree before your eyes*, and Isaiah likewise, *I have spread out my hands all the day unto a faithless and rebellious people.* Isaiah 65:2 But may we who worship this obtain a part in Christ the crucified. Amen.

Chapter 12. Concerning Worship towards the East.

It is not without reason or by chance that we worship towards the East. But seeing that we are composed of a visible and an invisible nature, that is to say, of a nature partly of spirit and partly of sense, we render also a twofold worship to the Creator; just as we sing both with our spirit and our bodily lips, and are baptized with both water and Spirit, and are united with the Lord in a twofold manner, being sharers in the mysteries and in the grace of the Spirit.

Since, therefore, God is spiritual light 1 John 1:5, and Christ is called in the Scriptures Sun of Righteousness Malachi 4:2 and Dayspring , the East is the direction that must be assigned to His worship. For everything good must be assigned to Him from Whom every good thing arises. Indeed the divine David also says, *Sing unto God, you kingdoms of the earth: O sing praises unto the Lord: to Him that rides upon the Heavens of heavens towards the East.* Moreover the Scripture also says, *And God planted a garden eastward in Eden; and there He put the man whom He had formed* Genesis 2:8: and when he had transgressed His command He expelled him and made him to dwell over against the delights of Paradise , which clearly is the West. So, then, we worship God seeking and striving after our old fatherland. Moreover the tent of Moses Leviticus 16:14 had its veil and mercy seat towards the East. Also the tribe of Judah as the most precious pitched their camp on the East. Numbers 2:3 Also in the celebrated temple of Solomon the Gate of the Lord was placed eastward. Moreover Christ, when He hung on the Cross, had His face turned towards the West, and so we worship, striving after Him. And when He was received again into Heaven He was borne towards the East, and thus His apostles worship Him, and thus He will come again in the way in which they beheld Him going towards Heaven Acts 1:11; as the Lord Himself said, *As the lightning comes out of the East and shines even unto the West, so also shall the coming of the Son of Man be Matthew 24:27 .*

So, then, in expectation of His coming we worship towards the East. But this tradition of the apostles is unwritten. For much that has been handed down to us by tradition is unwritten.

Chapter 13. Concerning the holy and immaculate Mysteries of the Lord.

God Who is good and altogether good and more than good, Who is goodness throughout, by reason of the exceeding riches of His goodness did not suffer Himself, that is His nature, only to be good, with no other to participate therein, but because of this He made first the spiritual and heavenly powers: next the visible and sensible universe: next man with his spiritual and sentient nature. All things, therefore, which he made, share in His goodness in respect of their existence. For He Himself is existence to all, since all things that are, are in Him Romans 11:36, not only because it was He that brought them out of nothing into being, but because His energy preserves and maintains all that He made: and in special the living creatures. For both in that they exist and in that they enjoy life they share in His goodness. But in truth those of them that have reason have a still greater share in that, both because of what has been already said and also because of the very reason which they possess. For they are somehow more dearly akin to Him, even though He is incomparably higher than they.

Man, however, being endowed with reason and free will, received the power of continuous union with God through his own choice, if indeed he should abide in goodness, that is in obedience to his Maker. Since, however, he transgressed the command of his Creator and became liable to death and corruption, the Creator and Maker of our race, because of His bowels of compassion, took on our likeness, becoming man in all things but without sin, and was united to our nature. Hebrews 2:17 For since He bestowed on us His own image and His own spirit and we did not keep them safe, He took Himself a share in our poor and weak nature, in order that He might cleanse us and make us incorruptible, and establish us once more as partakers of His divinity.

For it was fitting that not only the first-fruits of our nature should partake in the higher good but every man who wished it, and that a second birth should take place and that the nourishment should be new and suitable to the birth and thus the measure of perfection be attained. Through His birth, that is, His incarnation, and baptism and passion and resurrection, He delivered our nature from the sin of our first parent and death and corruption, and became the first-fruits of the resurrection, and made Himself the way and image and pattern, in order that we, too, following in His footsteps, may become by adoption what He is Himself by nature Romans 7:17, sons and heirs of God and joint heirs with Him. He gave us therefore, as I said, a second birth in order that, just as we who are born of Adam are in his image and are the heirs of the curse and corruption, so also being born of Him we may be in His likeness and heirs of His incorruption and blessing and glory.

Now seeing that this Adam is spiritual, it was meet that both the birth and likewise the food should be spiritual too, but since we are of a double and compound nature, it is meet that both the birth should be double and likewise the food compound. We were therefore given a birth by water and Spirit: I mean, by the holy baptism : and the food is the very bread of life, our Lord Jesus Christ, Who came down from heaven. John 6:48 For when He was about to take on Himself a voluntary death for our sakes, on the night on which He gave Himself up, He laid a new covenant on His holy disciples and apostles, and through them on all who believe in Him. In the upper chamber, then, of holy and illustrious Sion, after He had eaten the ancient Passover with His disciples and had fulfilled the ancient covenant, He washed His disciples' feet in token of the holy baptism. Then having broken bread He gave it to them saying, *Take, eat, this is My body broken for you for the remission of sins.* Likewise also He took the cup of wine and water and gave it to them saying, *Drink ye all of it: for this is My blood, the blood of the New Testament which is shed for you for the remission of sins. This do ye in remembrance of Me. For as often as you eat this bread and drink this cup, you do show the death of the Son of man and confess His resurrection until He come.*

If then the Word of God is quick and energising Hebrews 4:12, and the Lord did all that He willed ; if He said, Let there be light and there was light, let there be a firmament and there was a firmament ; if the heavens were established by the Word of the Lord and all the host of them by the breath of His mouth ; if the heaven and the earth, water and fire and air and the whole glory of these, and, in truth, this most noble creature, man, were perfected by the Word of the Lord; if God the Word of His own will became man and the pure and undefiled blood of the holy and ever-virginal One made His flesh without the aid of seed , can He not then make the bread His body and the wine and water His blood? He said in the beginning, *Let the earth bring forth grass* Genesis 1:11, and even until this present day, when the rain comes it brings forth its proper fruits, urged on and strengthened by the divine command. God said, *This is My body*, and *This is My blood, and this do ye in remembrance of Me.* And so it is at His omnipotent command *until He come:* for it was in this sense that He said until He come: and the overshadowing power of the Holy Spirit becomes through the invocation the rain to this new tillage. For just as God made all that He made by the energy of the Holy Spirit, so also now the energy of the Spirit performs those things that are supernatural and which it is not possible to comprehend unless by faith alone. *How shall this be*, said the Holy Virgin, *seeing I know not a man?* And the archangel Gabriel answered her: *The Holy Spirit shall come upon you, and the power of the Highest shall overshadow you.* Luke 1:34-35 And now you ask, how the bread became Christ's body and the wine and water Christ's blood. And I say unto you, The Holy Spirit is present and does those things which surpass reason and thought.

Further, bread and wine are employed: for God knows man's infirmity: for in general man turns away discontentedly from what is not well-worn by custom: and so with His usual indulgence He performs His supernatural works through familiar objects: and just as, in the case of baptism, since it is man's custom to wash himself with water and anoint himself with oil, He connected the grace of the Spirit with the oil and the water and made it the water of regeneration, in like manner since it is man's custom to eat and to drink water and wine , He connected His divinity with these and made them His body and blood in order that we may rise to what is supernatural through what is familiar and natural.

The body which is born of the holy Virgin is in truth body united with divinity, not that the body which was received up into the heavens descends, but that the bread itself and the wine are changed into God's body and blood.

But if you enquire how this happens, it is enough for you to learn that it was through the Holy Spirit, just as the Lord took on Himself flesh that subsisted in Him and was born of the holy Mother of God through the Spirit. And we know nothing further save that the Word of God is true and energises and is omnipotent, but the manner of this cannot be searched out. But one can put it well thus, that just as in nature the bread by the eating and the wine and the water by the drinking are changed into the body and blood of the eater and drinker, and do not become a different body from the former one, so the bread of the table and the wine and water are supernaturally changed by the invocation and presence of the Holy Spirit into the body and blood of Christ, and are not two but one and the same.

Wherefore to those who partake worthily with faith, it is for the remission of sins and for life everlasting and for the safeguarding of soul and body; but to those who partake unworthily without faith, it is for chastisement and punishment, just as also the death of the Lord became to those who believe life and incorruption for the enjoyment of eternal blessedness, while to those who do not believe and to the murderers of the Lord it is for everlasting chastisement and punishment.

The bread and the wine are not merely figures of the body and blood of Christ (God forbid!) but the deified body of the Lord itself: for the Lord has said, This is My body, not, this is a figure of My body: and My blood, not, a figure of My blood. And on a previous occasion He had said to the Jews, *Unless you eat the flesh of the Son of Man and drink His blood, you have no life in you. For My flesh is meat indeed and My blood is drink indeed.* And again, *He that eats Me, shall live* John 6:51-55.

Wherefore with all fear and a pure conscience and certain faith let us draw near and it will assuredly be to us as we believe, doubting nothing. Let us pay homage to it in all purity both of soul and body: for it is twofold. Let us draw near to it with an ardent desire, and with our hands held in the form of the cross let us receive the body of the Crucified One: and let us apply our eyes and lips and brows and partake of the divine coal, in order that the fire of the longing, that is in us, with the additional heat derived from the coal may utterly consume our sins and illumine our hearts, and that we may be inflamed and deified by the participation in the divine fire. Isaiah saw the coal. Isaiah 6:6 But coal is not plain wood but wood united with fire: in like manner also the bread of the communion is not plain bread but bread united with divinity. But a body which is united with divinity is not one nature, but has one nature belonging to the body and another belonging to the divinity that is united to it, so that the compound is not one nature but two.

With bread and wine Melchisedek, the priest of the most high God, received Abraham on his return from the slaughter of the Gentiles. Genesis 14:18 That table pre-imaged this mystical table, just as that priest was a type and image of Christ, the true high-priest. Leviticus xiv *For you are a priest for ever after the order of Melchisedek.* Of this bread the show-bread was an image. This surely is that pure and bloodless sacrifice which the Lord through the prophet said is offered to Him from the rising to the setting of the sun Malachi 1:11 .

The body and blood of Christ are making for the support of our soul and body, without being consumed or suffering corruption, not making for the draught (God forbid!) but for our being and preservation, a protection against all kinds of injury, a purging from all uncleanness: should one receive base gold, they purify it by the critical burning lest in the future we be condemned with this world. They purify from diseases and all kinds of calamities; according to the words of the divine Apostle 1 Corinthians 11:31-32, *For if we would judge ourselves, we should not be judged. But when we are judged, we are chastened of the Lord, that we should not be condemned with the world.* This too is what he says, *So that he that partakes of the body and blood of Christ unworthily, eats and drinks damnation to himself.* Being purified by this, we are united to the body of Christ and to His Spirit and become the body of Christ.

This bread is the first-fruits of the future bread which is ἐπιούσιος, i.e. necessary for existence. For the word ἐπιούσιον signifies either the future, that is Him Who is for a future age, or else Him of Whom we partake for the preservation of our essence. Whether then it is in this sense or that, it is fitting to speak so of the Lord's body. For the Lord's flesh is life-giving spirit because it was conceived of the life-giving Spirit. For what is born of the Spirit is spirit. But I do not say this to take away the nature of the body, but I wish to make clear its life-giving and divine power John 6:63 .

But if some persons called the bread and the wine antitypes of the body and blood of the Lord, as did the divinely inspired Basil, they said so not after the consecration but before the consecration, so calling the offering itself.

Participation is spoken of; for through it we partake of the divinity of Jesus. Communion, too, is spoken of, and it is an actual communion, because through it we have communion with Christ and share in His flesh and His divinity: yea, we have communion and are united with one another through it. For since we partake of one bread, we all become one body of Christ and one blood, and members one of another, being of one body with Christ.

With all our strength, therefore, let us beware lest we receive communion from or grant it to heretics; *Give not that which is holy unto the dogs, says the Lord, neither cast ye your pearls before swine* Matthew 7:6, lest we become partakers in their dishonour and condemnation. For if union is in truth with Christ and with one another, we are assuredly voluntarily united also with all those who partake with us. For this union is effected voluntarily and not against our inclination. *For we are all one body because we partake of the one bread*, as the divine Apostle says 1 Corinthians 10:17 .

Further, antitypes of future things are spoken of, not as though they were not in reality Christ's body and blood, but that now through them we partake of Christ's divinity, while then we shall partake mentally through the vision alone.

Chapter 14. Concerning our Lord's genealogy and concerning the holy Mother of God.

Concerning the holy and much-lauded ever-virgin one, Mary, the Mother of God, we have said something in the preceding chapters, bringing forward what was most opportune, viz., that strictly and truly she is and is called the Mother of God. Now let us fill up the blanks. For she being pre-ordained by the eternal prescient counsel of God and imaged forth and proclaimed in diverse images and discourses of the prophets through the Holy Spirit, sprang at the pre-determined time from the root of David, according to the promises that were made to him. *For the Lord has sworn, He says in truth to David, He will not turn from it: of the fruit of Your body will I set upon Your throne. And again, Once have I sworn by My holiness, that I will not lie unto David. His seed shall endure for ever, and His throne as the sun before Me. It shall be established for ever as the moon, and as a faithful witness in heaven.* And Isaiah says: *And there shall come out a rod out of the stem of Jesse and a branch shall grow out of his roots* Isaiah 11:1 .

But that Joseph is descended from the tribe of David is expressly demonstrated by Matthew and Luke, the most holy evangelists. But Matthew derives Joseph from David through Solomon, while Luke does so through Nathan; while over the holy Virgin's origin both pass in silence.

One ought to remember that it was not the custom of the Hebrews nor of the divine Scripture to give genealogies of women; and the law was to prevent one tribe seeking wives from another. And so since Joseph was descended from the tribe of David and was a just man (for this the divine Gospel testifies), he would not have espoused the holy Virgin contrary to the law; he would not have taken her unless she had been of the same tribe. It was sufficient, therefore, to demonstrate the descent of Joseph.

One ought also to observe this, that the law was that when a man died without seed, this man's brother should take to wife the wife of the dead man and raise up seed to his brother. Deuteronomy 25:5 The offspring, therefore, belonged by nature to the second, that is, to him that begot it, but by law to the dead.

Born then of the line of Nathan, the son of David, Levi begot Melchi and Panther: Panther begot Barpanther, so called. This Barpanther begot Joachim: Joachim begot the holy Mother of God . And of the line of Solomon, the son of David, Mathan had a wife of whom he begot Jacob. Now on the death of Mathan, Melchi, of the tribe of Nathan, the son of Levi and brother of Panther, married the wife of Mathan, Jacob's mother, of whom he begot Heli. Therefore Jacob and Heli became brothers on the mother's side, Jacob being of the tribe of Solomon and Heli of the tribe of Nathan. Then Heli of the tribe of Nathan died childless, and Jacob his brother, of the tribe of Solomon, took his wife and raised up seed to his brother and begot Joseph. Joseph, therefore, is by nature the son of Jacob, of the line of Solomon, but by law he is the son of Heli of the line of Nathan.

Joachim then took to wife that revered and praiseworthy woman, Anna. But just as the earlier Anna 1 Samuel 1:2, who was barren, bore Samuel by prayer and by promise, so also this Anna by supplication and promise from God bare the Mother of God in order that she might not even in this be behind the matrons of fame. Accordingly it was grace (for this is the interpretation of Anna) that bore the lady: (for she became truly the Lady of all created things in becoming the Mother of the Creator). Further, Joachim was born in the house of the *Probatica* , and was brought up to the temple. Then planted in the House of God and increased by the Spirit, like a fruitful olive tree, she became the home of every virtue, turning her mind away from every secular and carnal desire, and thus keeping her soul as well as her body virginal, as was meet for her who was to receive God into her bosom: for as He is holy, He finds rest among the holy. Thus, therefore, she strove after holiness, and was declared a holy and wonderful temple fit for the most high God.

Moreover, since the enemy of our salvation was keeping a watchful eye on virgins, according to the prophecy of Isaiah, who said, *Behold a virgin shall conceive and bare a Son and shall call His name Emmanuel, which is, being interpreted, 'God with us* ,' in order that *he who takes the wise in their own craftiness* may deceive him who always glories in his wisdom, the maiden is given in marriage to Joseph by the priests, a new book to him who is versed in letters Isaiah 29:11: but the marriage was both the protection of the virgin and the delusion of him who was keeping a watchful eye on virgins. But when the fullness of time had come, the messenger of the Lord was sent to her, with the good news of our Lord's conception. And thus she conceived the Son of God, the hypostatic power of the Father, *not of the will of the flesh nor of the will of man* John 1:13, that is to say, by connection and seed, but by the good pleasure of the Father and co-operation of the Holy Spirit. She ministered to the Creator in that He was created, to the Fashioner in that He was fashioned, and to the Son of God and God in that He was made flesh and became man from her pure and immaculate flesh and blood, satisfying the debt of the first mother. For just as the latter was formed from Adam without connection, so also did the former bring forth the new Adam, who was brought forth in accordance with the laws of parturition and above the nature of generation.

For He who was of the Father, yet without mother, was born of woman without a father's co-operation. And so far as He was born of woman, His birth was in accordance with the laws of parturition, while so far as He had no father, His birth was above the nature of generation: and in that it was at the usual time (for He was born on the completion of the ninth month when the tenth was just beginning), His birth was in accordance with the laws of parturition, while in that it was painless it was above the laws of generation. For, as pleasure did not precede it, pain did not follow it, according to the prophet who says, *Before she travailed, she brought forth, and again, before her pain came she was delivered of a man-child.* Isaiah 66:7 The Son of God incarnate, therefore, was born of her, not a divinely-inspired man but God incarnate; not a prophet anointed with energy but by the presence of the anointing One in His completeness, so that the Anointer became man and the Anointed God, not by a change of nature but by union in subsistence. For the Anointer and the Anointed were one and the same, anointing in the capacity of God Himself as man. Must there not therefore be a Mother of God who bore God incarnate? Assuredly she who played the part of the Creator's servant and mother is in all strictness and truth in reality God's Mother and Lady and Queen over all created things. But just as He who was conceived kept her who conceived still virgin, in like manner also He who was born preserved her virginity intact, only passing through her and keeping her closed. Ezekiel 44:2 The conception, indeed, was through the sense of hearing, but the birth through the usual path by which children come, although some tell tales of His birth through the side of the Mother of God. For it was not impossible for Him to have come by this gate, without injuring her seal in anyway.

The ever-virgin One thus remains even after the birth still virgin, having never at any time up till death consorted with a man. For although it is written, *And knew her not till she had brought forth her first-born Son* Matthew 1:25, yet note that he who is first-begotten is first-born even if he is only-begotten. For the word first-born means that he was born first but does not at all suggest the birth of others. And the word till signifies the limit of the appointed time but does not exclude the time thereafter. For the Lord says, *And lo, I am with you always, even unto the end of the world* , not meaning thereby that He will be separated from us after the completion of the age. The divine apostle, indeed, says, *And so shall we ever be with the Lord* 1 Thessalonians 4:17, meaning after the general resurrection.

For could it be possible that she, who had borne God and from experience of the subsequent events had come to know the miracle, should receive the embrace of a man. God forbid! It is not the part of a chaste mind to think such thoughts, far less to commit such acts.

But this blessed woman, who was deemed worthy of gifts that are supernatural, suffered those pains, which she escaped at the birth, in the hour of the passion, enduring from motherly sympathy the rending of the bowels, and when she beheld Him, Whom she knew to be God by the manner of His generation, killed as a malefactor, her thoughts pierced her as a sword, and this is the meaning of this verse: *Yea, a sword shall pierce through your own soul also* Luke 2:35. But the joy of the resurrection transforms the pain, proclaiming Him, Who died in the flesh, to be God.

Chapter 15. Concerning the honour due to the Saints and their remains.

To the saints honour must be paid as friends of Christ, as sons and heirs of God: in the words of John the theologian and evangelist, *As many as received Him, to them gave He power to became sons of God.* John 1:12 *So that they are no longer servants, but sons: and if sons, also heirs, heirs of God and joint heirs with Christ* : and the Lord in the holy Gospels says to His apostles, *You are My friends* John 15:14 . *Henceforth I call you not servants, for the servant knows not what his lord does.* And further, if the Creator and Lord of all things is called also King of Kings and Lord of Lords Revelation 19:16 and God of Gods, surely also the saints are gods and lords and kings. For of these God is and is called God and Lord and King. *For I am the God of Abraham,* He said to Moses, *the God of Isaac and the God of Jacob.* Exodus 3:6 And God made Moses a god to Pharaoh. Now I mean gods and kings and lords not in nature, but as rulers and masters of their passions, and as preserving a truthful likeness to the divine image according to which they were made (for the image of a king is also called king), and as being united to God of their own free-will and receiving Him as an indweller and becoming by grace through participation with Him what He is Himself by nature. Surely, then, the worshippers and friends and sons of God are to be held in honour? For the honour shown to the most thoughtful of fellow-servants is a proof of good feeling towards the common Master.

These are made treasuries and pure habitations of God: *For I will dwell in them,* said God, *and walk in them, and I will be their God.* The divine Scripture likewise says that the souls of the just are in God's hand Wisdom 3:1 and death cannot lay hold of them. For death is rather the sleep of the saints than their death. *For they travailed in this life and shall to the end* , and *Precious in the sight of the Lord is the death of His saints.* What then, is more precious than to be in the hand of God? For God is Life and Light, and those who are in God's hand are in life and light.

Further, that God dwelt even in their bodies in spiritual wise , the Apostle tells us, saying, *Do you not know that your bodies are the temples of the Holy Spirit dwelling in you?* 1 Corinthians 3:16, and The *Lord is that Spirit* 2 Corinthians 3:17, and *If any one destroy the temple of God, him will God destroy.* 1 Corinthians 3:17 Surely, then, we must ascribe honour to the living temples of God, the living tabernacles of God. These while they lived stood with confidence before God.

The Master Christ made the remains of the saints to be fountains of salvation to us, pouring forth manifold blessings and abounding in oil of sweet fragrance: and let no one disbelieve this. For if water burst in the desert from the steep and solid rock at God's will Exodus 17:6 and from the jaw-bone of an ass to quench Samson's thirst Judges 15:17, is it incredible that fragrant oil should burst forth from the martyrs' remains? By no means, at least to those who know the power of God and the honour which He accords His saints.

In the law every one who touches a dead body was considered impure Numbers 19:11, but these are not dead. For from the time when He that is Himself life and the Author of life was reckoned among the dead, we do not call those dead who have fallen asleep in the hope of the resurrection and in faith on Him. For how could a dead body work miracles? How, therefore, are demons driven off by them, diseases dispelled, sick persons made well, the blind restored to sight, lepers purified, temptations and troubles overcome, and how does every good gift from the Father of lights James 1:17 come down through them to those who pray with sure faith? How much labour would you not undergo to find a patron to introduce you to a mortal king and speak to him on your behalf? Are not those, then, worthy of honour who are the patrons of the whole race, and make intercession to God for us? Yea, verily, we ought to give honour to them by raising temples to God in their name, bringing them fruit-offerings, honouring their memories and taking spiritual delight in them, in order that the joy of those who call on us may be ours, that in our attempts at worship we may not on the contrary cause them offense. For those who worship God will take pleasure in those things whereby God is worshipped, while His shield-bearers will be wrath at those things wherewith God is angry. In psalms and hymns and spiritual songs Ephesians 5:19, in contrition and in pity for the needy, let us believers worship the saints, as God also is most worshipped in such wise. Let us raise monuments to them and visible images, and let us ourselves become, through imitation of their virtues, living monuments and images of them. Let us give honour to her who bore God as being strictly and truly the Mother of God.

Let us honour also the prophet John as forerunner and baptist , as apostle and martyr, *For among them that are born of women there has not risen a greater than John the Baptist* Matthew 11:11, as says the Lord, and he became the first to proclaim the Kingdom. Let us honour the apostles as the Lord's brothers, who saw Him face to face and ministered to His passion, *for whom God the Father did foreknow He also did predestinate to be conformed to the image of His Son* Romans 8:29, *first apostles, second prophets* 1 Corinthians 12:24, *third pastors and teachers.* Ephesians 4:11 Let us also honour the martyrs of the Lord chosen out of every class, as soldiers of Christ who have drunk His cup and were then baptized with the baptism of His life-bringing death, to be partakers of His passion and glory: of whom the leader is Stephen, the first deacon of Christ and apostle and first martyr. Also let us honour our holy fathers, the God-possessed ascetics, whose struggle was the longer and more toilsome one of the conscience: *who wandered about in sheepskins and goatskins, being destitute, afflicted, tormented; they wandered in deserts and in mountains and in dens and caves of the earth, of whom the world was not worthy.* Hebrews 11:37-38 Let us honour those who were prophets before grace, the patriarchs and just men who foretold the Lord's coming. Let us carefully review the life of these men, and let us emulate their faith and love and hope and zeal and way of life, and endurance of sufferings and patience even to blood, in order that we may be sharers with them in their crowns of glory.

Chapter 16. Concerning Images.

But since some find fault with us for worshipping and honouring the image of our Saviour and that of our Lady, and those, too, of the rest of the saints and servants of Christ, let them remember that in the beginning God created man after His own image. Genesis 1:26 On what grounds, then, do we show reverence to each other unless because we are made after God's image? For as Basil, that much-versed expounder of divine things, says, the honour given to the image passes over to the prototype. Now a prototype is that which is imaged, from which the derivative is obtained. Why was it that the Mosaic people honoured on all hands the tabernacle Exodus 33:10 which bore an image and type of heavenly things, or rather of the whole creation? God indeed said to Moses, *Look that thou make them after their pattern which was showed you in the mount.* The Cherubim, too, which o'ershadow the mercy seat, are they not the work of men's hands Exodus 25:18? What, further, is the celebrated temple at Jerusalem? Is it not hand-made and fashioned by the skill of men 1 Kings viii?

Moreover the divine Scripture blames those who worship graven images, but also those who sacrifice to demons. The Greeks sacrificed and the Jews also sacrificed: but the Greeks to demons and the Jews to God. And the sacrifice of the Greeks was rejected and condemned, but the sacrifice of the just was very acceptable to God. For Noah sacrificed, and *God smelled a sweet savour* Genesis 8:21, receiving the fragrance of the right choice and good-will towards Him. And so the graven images of the Greeks, since they were images of deities, were rejected and forbidden.

But besides this who can make an imitation of the invisible, incorporeal, uncircumscribed, formless God? Therefore to give form to the Deity is the height of folly and impiety. And hence it is that in the Old Testament the use of images was not common. But after God in His bowels of pity became in truth man for our salvation, not as He was seen by Abraham in the semblance of a man, nor as He was seen by the prophets, but in being truly man, and after He lived upon the earth and dwelt among men Baruch 3:38, worked miracles, suffered, was crucified, rose again and was taken back to Heaven, since all these things actually took place and were seen by men, they were written for the remembrance and instruction of us who were not alive at that time in order that though we saw not, we may still, hearing and believing, obtain the blessing of the Lord. But seeing that not every one has a knowledge of letters nor time for reading, the Fathers gave their sanction to depicting these events on images as being acts of great heroism, in order that they should form a concise memorial of them. Often, doubtless, when we have not the Lord's passion in mind and see the image of Christ's crucifixion, His saving passion is brought back to remembrance, and we fall down and worship not the material but that which is imaged: just as we do not worship the material of which the Gospels are made, nor the material of the Cross, but that which these typify. For wherein does the cross, that typifies the Lord, differ from a cross that does not do so? It is just the same also in the case of the Mother of the Lord. For the honour which we give to her is referred to Him Who was made of her incarnate. And similarly also the brave acts of holy men stir us up to be brave and to emulate and imitate their valour and to glorify God. For as we said, the honour that is given to the best of fellow-servants is a proof of good-will towards our common Lady, and the honour rendered to the image passes over to the prototype. But this is an unwritten tradition , just as is also the worshipping towards the East and the worship of the Cross, and very many other similar things.

A certain tale , too, is told , how that when Augarus was king over the city of the Edessenes, he sent a portrait painter to paint a likeness of the Lord, and when the painter could not paint because of the brightness that shone from His countenance, the Lord Himself put a garment over His own divine and life-giving face and impressed on it an image of Himself and sent this to Augarus, to satisfy thus his desire.

Moreover that the Apostles handed down much that was unwritten, Paul, the Apostle of the Gentiles, tells us in these words: *Therefore, brethren, stand fast and*

hold the traditions which you have been taught of us, whether by word or by epistle.
2 Thessalonians 2:15 And to the Corinthians he writes, *Now I praise you, brethren, that you remember me in all things, and keep the traditions as I have delivered them to you* 1 Corinthians 11:2 .

Chapter 17. Concerning Scripture.

It is one and the same God Whom both the Old and the New Testament proclaim, Who is praised and glorified in the Trinity: *I have come*, says the Lord, *not to destroy the law but to fulfil it.* Matthew 5:17 For He Himself worked out our salvation for which all Scripture and all mystery exists. And again, *Search the Scriptures for they are they that testify of Me.* John 5:39 And the Apostle says, *God, Who at sundry times and in diverse manners spoke in time past unto the fathers by the prophets, has in these last days spoken unto us by His Son.* Hebrews 1:1-2 Through the Holy Spirit, therefore, both the law and the prophets, the evangelists and apostles and pastors and teachers, spoke.

All Scripture, then, is *given by inspiration of God and is also assuredly profitable.* 2 Timothy 3:16 Wherefore to search the Scriptures is a work most fair and most profitable for souls. For just as the tree planted by the channels of waters, so also the soul watered by the divine Scripture is enriched and gives fruit in its season , viz. orthodox belief, and is adorned with evergreen leafage, I mean, actions pleasing to God. For through the Holy Scriptures we are trained to action that is pleasing to God, and untroubled contemplation. For in these we find both exhortation to every virtue and dissuasion from every vice. If, therefore, we are lovers of learning, we shall also be learned in many things. For by care and toil and the grace of God the Giver, all things are accomplished. *For every one that asks receives, and he that seeks finds, and to him that knocks it shall be opened.* Luke 11:10 Wherefore let us knock at that very fair garden of the Scriptures, so fragrant and sweet and blooming, with its varied sounds of spiritual and divinely-inspired birds ringing all round our ears, laying hold of our hearts, comforting the mourner, pacifying the angry and filling him with joy everlasting: which sets our mind on the gold-gleaming, brilliant back of the divine dove , whose bright pinions bear up to the only-begotten Son and Heir of the Husbandman Matthew 21:37 of that spiritual Vineyard and bring us through Him to the Father of Lights. James 1:17 But let us not knock carelessly but rather zealously and constantly: lest knocking we grow weary. For thus it will be opened to us. If we read once or twice and do not understand what we read, let us not grow weary, but let us persist, let us talk much, let us enquire. For *ask your Father*, he says, *and He will show you: your elders and they will tell you.* Deuteronomy 32:7 For *there is not in every man that knowledge.* 1 Corinthians 8:7 Let us draw of the fountain of the garden perennial and purest waters springing into life eternal. John 4:14 Here let us luxuriate, let us revel insatiate: for the Scriptures possess inexhaustible grace.

But if we are able to pluck anything profitable from outside sources, there is nothing to forbid that. Let us become tried money-dealers, heaping up the true and pure gold and discarding the spurious. Let us keep the fairest sayings but let us throw to the dogs absurd gods and strange myths: for we might prevail most mightily against them through themselves.

Observe, further , that there are two and twenty books of the Old Testament, one for each letter of the Hebrew tongue. For there are twenty-two letters of which five are double, and so they come to be twenty-seven. For the letters Caph, Mem, Nun, Pe , Sade are double. And thus the number of the books in this way is twenty-two, but is found to be twenty-seven because of the double character of five. For Ruth is joined on to Judges, and the Hebrews count them one book: the first and second books of Kings are counted one: and so are the third and fourth books of Kings: and also the first and second of Paraleipomena: and the first and second of Esdra. In this way, then, the books are collected together in four Pentateuchs and two others remain over, to form thus the canonical books. Five of them are of the Law, viz. Genesis, Exodus, Leviticus, Numbers, Deuteronomy. This which is the code of the Law, constitutes the first Pentateuch. Then comes another Pentateuch, the so-called Grapheia , or as they are called by some, the Hagiographa, which are the following: Jesus the Son of Nave , Judges along with Ruth, first and second Kings, which are one book, third and fourth Kings, which are one book, and the two books of the Paraleipomena which are one book. This is the second Pentateuch. The third Pentateuch is the books in verse, viz. Job, Psalms, Proverbs of Solomon, Ecclesiastes of Solomon and the Song of Songs of Solomon. The fourth Pentateuch is the Prophetical books, viz the twelve prophets constituting one book, Isaiah, Jeremiah, Ezekiel, Daniel. Then come the two books of Esdra made into one, and Esther. There are also the Panaretus, that is the Wisdom of Solomon, and the Wisdom of Jesus, which was published in Hebrew by the father of Sirach, and afterwards translated into Greek by his grandson, Jesus, the Son of Sirach. These are virtuous and noble, but are not counted nor were they placed in the ark.

The New Testament contains four gospels, that according to Matthew, that according to Mark, that according to Luke, that according to John: the Acts of the Holy Apostles by Luke the Evangelist: seven catholic epistles, viz. one of James, two of Peter, three of John, one of Jude: fourteen letters of the Apostle Paul: the Revelation of John the Evangelist: the Canons of the holy apostles , by Clement.

Chapter 18. Regarding the things said concerning Christ.

The things said concerning Christ fall into four generic modes. For some fit Him even before the incarnation, others in the union, others after the union, and others after the resurrection. Also of those that refer to the period before the incarnation there are six modes: for some of them declare the union of nature and the identity in essence with the Father, as this, *I and My Father are one* John 10:30: also this, *He that has seen Me has seen the Father*: and this, *Who being in the form of God* Philippians 2:6, and so forth. Others declare the perfection of subsistence, as these, *Son of God*, and *the Express Image of His person* Hebrews 1:3, and *Messenger of great counsel, Wonderful Counsellor* Isaiah 9:6, and the like.

Again, others declare the indwelling of the subsistences in one another, as, *I am in the Father and the Father in Me* John 14:10; and the inseparable foundation , as, for instance, the Word, Wisdom, Power, Effulgence. For the word is inseparably established in the mind (and it is the essential mind that I mean), and so also is wisdom, and power in him that is powerful, and effulgence in the light, all springing forth from these.

And others make known the fact of His origin from the Father as cause, for instance *My Father is greater than I.* John 14:28 For from Him He derives both His being and all that He has : His being was by generative and not by creative means, as, *I came forth from the Father and have come* John 16:28, and *I live by the Father* . But all that He has is not His by free gift or by teaching, but in a causal sense, as, *The Son can do nothing of Himself but what He sees the Father do.* For if the Father is not, neither is the Son. For the Son is of the Father and in the Father and with the Father, and not after the Father. In like manner also what He does is of Him and with Him. For there is one and the same, not similar but the same, will and energy and power in the Father, Son and Holy Spirit.

Moreover, other things are said as though the Father's good-will was fulfilled through His energy, and not as through an instrument or a servant, but as through His essential and hypostatic Word and Wisdom and Power, because but one action is observed in Father and Son, as for example, *All things were made by Him* John 11:42, and *He sent His Word and healed them* , and *That they may believe that You have sent Me* John 17:2 .

Some, again, have a prophetic sense, and of these some are in the future tense: for instance, *He shall come openly* , and this from Zechariah, *Behold, your King comes unto you* Zechariah 9:9, and this from Micah, *Behold, the Lord comes out of His place and will come down and tread upon the high places of the earth.* Micah 1:3 But others, though future, are put in the past tense, as, for instance, *This is our God: Therefore He was seen upon the earth and dwelt among men* Baruch 3:38, and *The Lord created me in the beginning of His ways for His works* Proverbs 8:22, and *Wherefore God, your God, anointed you with the oil of gladness above your fellows* , and such like.

The things said, then, that refer to the period before the union will be applicable to Him even after the union: but those that refer to the period after the union will not be applicable at all before the union, unless indeed in a prophetic sense, as we said. Those that refer to the time of the union have three modes. For when our discourse deals with the higher aspect, we speak of the deification of the flesh, and His assumption of the Word and exceeding exaltation, and so forth, making manifest the riches that are added to the flesh from the union and natural conjunction with the most high God the Word. And when our discourse deals with the lower aspect, we speak of the incarnation of God the Word, His becoming man, His emptying of Himself, His poverty, His humility. For these and such like are imposed upon the Word and God through His admixture with humanity. When again we keep both sides in view at the same time, we speak of union, community, anointing, natural conjunction, conformation and the like. The former two modes, then, have their reason in this third mode. For through the union it is made clear what either has obtained from the intimate junction with and permeation through the other. For through the union in subsistence the flesh is said to be deified and to become God and to be equally God with the Word; and God the Word is said to be made flesh, and to become man, and is called creature and last Isaiah 48:12: not in the sense that the two natures are converted into one compound nature (for it is not possible for the opposite natural qualities to exist at the same time in one nature) , but in the sense that the two natures are united in subsistence and permeate one another without confusion or transmutation. The permeation moreover did not come of the flesh but of the divinity: for it is impossible that the flesh should permeate through the divinity: but the divine nature once permeating through the flesh gave also to the flesh the same ineffable power of permeation ; and this indeed is what we call union.

Note, too, that in the case of the first and second modes of those that belong to the period of the union, reciprocation is observed. For when we speak about the flesh, we use the terms deification and assumption of the Word and exceeding exaltation and anointing. For these are derived from divinity, but are observed in connection with the flesh. And when we speak about the Word, we use the terms emptying, incarnation, becoming man, humility and the like: and these, as we said, are imposed on the Word and God through the flesh. For He endured these things in person of His own free-will.

Of the things that refer to the period after the union there are three modes. The first declares His divine nature, as, *I am in the Father and the Father in Me* John 14:1, and *I and the Father are one* : and all those things which are affirmed of Him before His assumption of humanity, these will be affirmed of Him even after His assumption of humanity, with this exception, that He did not assume the flesh and its natural properties.

The second declares His human nature, as, *Now ye seek to kill Me, a man that has told you the truth* , and *Even so must the Son of Man be lifted up* , and the like.

Further, of the statements made and written about Christ the Saviour after the manner of men, whether they deal with sayings or actions, there are six modes. For some of them were done or said naturally in accordance with the incarnation; for instance, His birth from a virgin, His growth and progress with age, His hunger, thirst, weariness, fear, sleep, piercing with nails, death and all such like natural and innocent passions. For in all these there is a mixture of the divine and human, although they are held to belong in reality to the body, the divine suffering none of these, but procuring through them our salvation.

Others are of the nature of ascription , as Christ's question, *Where have ye laid Lazarus* John 11:34? His running to the fig-tree, His shrinking, that is, His drawing back, His praying, and His making *as though He would have gone further* Luke 24:28 For neither as God nor as man was He in need of these or similar things, but only because His form was that of a man as necessity and expediency demanded. For example, the praying was to show that He is not opposed to God, for He gives honour to the Father as the cause of Himself : and the question was not put in ignorance but to show that He is in truth man as well as God ; and the drawing back is to teach us not to be impetuous nor to give ourselves up.

Others again are said in the manner of association and relation , as, *My God, My God, why have You forsaken Me* Matthew 27:46 ? and *He has made Him to be sin for us, Who knew no sin* 2 Corinthians 5:21 , *and being made a curse for us* Galatians 3:13; also, *Then shall the Son also Himself be subject unto Him that put all things under Him* 1 Corinthians 15:28 For neither as God nor as man was He ever forsaken by the Father, nor did He become sin or a curse, nor did He require to be made subject to the Father. For as God He is equal to the Father and not opposed to Him nor subjected to Him; and as God, He was never at any time disobedient to His Begetter to make it necessary for Him to make Him subject. Appropriating, then, our person and ranking Himself with us, He used these words. For we are bound in the fetters of sin and the curse as faithless and disobedient, and therefore forsaken.

Others are said by reason of distinction in thought. For if you divide in thought things that are inseparable in actual truth, to cut the flesh from the Word, the terms 'servant' and 'ignorant' are used of Him, for indeed He was of a subject and ignorant nature, and except that it was united with God the Word, His flesh was servile and ignorant. But because of the union in subsistence with God the Word it was neither servile nor ignorant. In this way, too, He called the Father His God.

Others again are for the purpose of revealing Him to us and strengthening our faith, as, *And now, O Father, glorify Thou Me with the glory which I had with You, before the world was.* John 17:5 For He Himself was glorified and is glorified, but His glory was not manifested nor confirmed to us. Also that which the apostle said, *Declared to be the Son of God with power, according to the spirit of holiness, by the resurrection from the dead.* Romans 1:4 For by the miracles and the resurrection and the coming of the Holy Spirit it was manifested and confirmed to the world that He is the Son of God. And this too Luke 2:40, *The Child grew in wisdom and grace.*

Others again have reference to His appropriation of the personal life of the Jews, in numbering Himself among the Jews, as He says to the Samaritan woman, *You worship ye know not what: we know what we worship, far salvation is of the Jews* John 4:22 .

The third mode is one which declares the one subsistence and brings out the dual nature: for instance, *And I live by the Father: so he that eats Me, even he shall live by Me.* And this: *I go to My Father and you see Me no more.* And this: *They would not have crucified the Lord of Glory.* 1 Corinthians 2:8 And this: *And no man has ascended up to heaven but He that came down from heaven, even the Son of Man which is in heaven* John 3:13, and such like.

Again of the affirmations that refer to the period after the resurrection some are suitable to God, as, *Baptizing them in the name of the Father, and of the Son, and of the Holy Ghost* Matthew 28:19, for here 'Son' is clearly used as God; also this, *And lo, I am with you always, even unto the end of the world* , and other similar ones. For He is with us as God. Others are suitable to man, as, *They held Him by the feet* , and *There they will see Me* , and so forth.

Further, of those referring to the period after the Resurrection that are suitable to man there are different modes. For some did actually take place, yet not according to nature , but according to dispensation, in order to confirm the fact that the very body, which suffered, rose again; such are the weals, the eating and the drinking after the resurrection. Others took place actually and naturally, as changing from place to place without trouble and passing in through closed gates. Others have the character of simulation , as, *He made as though He would have gone further.* Luke 24:28 Others are appropriate to the double nature, as, *I ascend unto My Father and your Father, and My God and your God* John 20:17, and *The King of Glory shall come in* , and *He sat down on the right hand of the majesty on High.* Hebrews 1:3 Finally others are to be understood as though He were ranking Himself with us, in the manner of separation in pure thought, as, *My God and your God* John 20:17 .

Those then that are sublime must be assigned to the divine nature, which is superior to passion and body: and those that are humble must be ascribed to the human nature; and those that are common must be attributed to the compound, that is, the one Christ, Who is God and man. And it should be understood that both belong to one and the same Jesus Christ, our Lord. For if we know what is proper to each, and perceive that both are performed by one and the same, we shall have the true faith and shall not go astray. And from all these the difference between the united natures is recognised, and the fact that, as the most godly Cyril says, they are not identical in the natural quality of their divinity and humanity. But yet there is but one Son and Christ and Lord: and as He is one, He has also but one person, the unity in subsistence being in nowise broken up into parts by the recognition of the difference of the natures.

Chapter 19. That God is not the cause of evils.

It is to be observed that it is the custom in the Holy Scripture to speak of God's permission as His energy, as when the apostle says in the Epistle to the Romans, *Hath not the potter power over the clay, of the same lump to make one vessel unto honour and another unto dishonour?* And for this reason, that He Himself makes this or that. For He is Himself alone the Maker of all things; yet it is not He Himself that fashions noble or ignoble things, but the personal choice of each one. And this is manifest from what the same Apostle says in the Second Epistle to Timothy, *In a great house there are not only vessels of gold and of silver, but also of wood and of earth: and some to honour and some to dishonour. If a man therefore purge himself from these, he shall be a vessel unto honour sanctified, and meet for the master's use, and prepared unto every good work.* 2 Timothy 2:20-21 And it is evident that the purification must be voluntary: for *if a man*, he says, *purge himself.* And the consequent antistrophe responds, If a man purge not himself he will be a vessel to dishonour, unmeet for the master's use and fit only to be broken in pieces. Wherefore this passage that we have quoted and this, *God has concluded them all in unbelief* Romans 11:32, and this, *God has given them the spirit of slumber, eyes that they should not see, and ears that they should not hear*, all these must be understood not as though God Himself were energising, but as though God were permitting, both because of free-will and because goodness knows no compulsion.

His permission, therefore, is usually spoken of in the Holy Scripture as His energy and work. Nay, even when He says that *God creates evil things*, and that *there is no evil in a city that the Lord has not done*, he does not mean by these words Amos 3:6 that the Lord is the cause of evil, but the word 'evil' is used in two ways, with two meanings. For sometimes it means what is evil by nature, and this is the opposite of virtue and the will of God: and sometimes it means that which is evil and oppressive to our sensation, that is to say, afflictions and calamities. Now these are seemingly evil because they are painful, but in reality are good. For to those who understand they became ambassadors of conversion and salvation. The Scripture says that of these God is the Author.

It is, moreover, to be observed that of these, too, we are the cause: for involuntary evils are the offspring of voluntary ones.

This also should be recognised, that it is usual in the Scriptures for some things that ought to be considered as effects to be stated in a causal sense , as, *Against You, You only, have I sinned and done this evil in Your sight, that You might be justified when You speak, and prevail when You judge.* For the sinner did not sin in order that God might prevail, nor again did God require our sin in order that He might by it be revealed as victor. For above comparison He wins the victor's prize against all, even against those who are sinless, being Maker, incomprehensible, uncreated, and possessing natural and not adventitious glory. But it is because when we sin God is not unjust in His anger against us; and when He pardons the penitent He is shown victor over our wickedness. But it is not for this that we sin, but because the thing so turns out. It is just as if one were sitting at work and a friend stood near by, and one said, My friend came in order that I might do no work that day. The friend, however, was not present in order that the man should do no work, but such was the result. For being occupied with receiving his friend he did not work. These things, too, are spoken of as effects because affairs so turned out. Moreover, God does not wish that He alone should be just, but that all should, so far as possible, be made like Him.

Chapter 20. That there are not two Kingdoms.

That there are not two kingdoms , one good and one bad, we shall see from this. For good and evil are opposed to one another and mutually destructive, and cannot exist in one another or with one another. Each of them, therefore, in its own division will belong to the whole, and first they will be circumscribed, not by the whole alone but also each of them by part of the whole.

Next I ask , who it is that assigns to each its place. For they will not affirm that they have come to a friendly agreement with, or been reconciled to, one another. For evil is not evil when it is at peace with, and reconciled to, goodness, nor is goodness good when it is on amicable terms with evil. But if He Who has marked off to each of these its own sphere of action is something different from them, He must the rather be God.

One of two things indeed is necessary, either that they come in contact with and destroy one another, or that there exists some intermediate place where neither goodness nor evil exists, separating both from one another, like a partition. And so there will be no longer two but three kingdoms.

Again, one of these alternatives is necessary, either that they are at peace, which is quite incompatible with evil (for that which is at peace is not evil), or they are at strife, which is incompatible with goodness (for that which is at strife is not perfectly good), or the evil is at strife and the good does not retaliate, but is destroyed by the evil, or they are ever in trouble and distress , which is not a mark of goodness. There is, therefore, but one kingdom, delivered from all evil.

But if this is so, they say, whence comes evil ? For it is quite impossible that evil should originate from goodness. We answer then, that evil is nothing else than absence of goodness and a lapsing from what is natural into what is unnatural: for nothing evil is natural. For all things, whatsoever God made, are very good Genesis 1:31, so far as they were made: if, therefore, they remain just as they were created, they are very good, but when they voluntarily depart from what is natural and turn to what is unnatural, they slip into evil.

By nature, therefore, all things are servants of the Creator and obey Him. Whenever, then, any of His creatures voluntarily rebels and becomes disobedient to his Maker, he introduces evil into himself. For evil is not any essence nor a property of essence, but an accident, that is, a voluntary deviation from what is natural into what is unnatural, which is sin.

Whence, then, comes sin ? It is an invention of the free-will of the devil. Is the devil, then, evil? In so far as he was brought into existence he is not evil but good. For he was created by his Maker a bright and very brilliant angel, endowed with free-will as being rational. But he voluntarily departed from the virtue that is natural and came into the darkness of evil, being far removed from God, Who alone is good and can give life and light. For from Him every good thing derives its goodness, and so far as it is separated from Him in will (for it is not in place), it falls into evil.

Chapter 21. The purpose for which God in His foreknowledge created persons who would sin and not repent.

God in His goodness brought what exists into being out of nothing, and has foreknowledge of what will exist in the future. If, therefore, they were not to exist in the future, they would neither be evil in the future nor would they be foreknown. For knowledge is of what exists and foreknowledge is of what will surely exist in the future. For simple being comes first and then good or evil being. But if the very existence of those, who through the goodness of

God are in the future to exist, were to be prevented by the fact that they were to become evil of their own choice, evil would have prevailed over the goodness of God. Wherefore God makes all His works good, but each becomes of its own choice good or evil. Although, then, the Lord said, *Good were it for that man that he had never been born* Mark 14:21, He said it in condemnation not of His own creation but of the evil which His own creation had acquired by his own choice and through his own heedlessness. For the heedlessness that marks man's judgment made His Creator's beneficence of no profit to him. It is just as if any one, when he had obtained riches and dominion from a king, were to lord it over his benefactor, who, when he has worsted him, will punish him as he deserves, if he should see him keeping hold of the sovereignty to the end.

Chapter 22. Concerning the law of God and the law of sin.

The Deity is good and more than good, and so is His will. For that which God wishes is good. Moreover the precept, which teaches this, is law, that we, holding by it, may walk in light 1 John 1:7: and the transgression of this precept is sin, and this continues to exist on account of the assault of the devil and our unconstrained and voluntary reception of it. Romans 7:23 And this, too, is called law Romans 7:25 .

And so the law of God, settling in our mind, draws it towards itself and pricks our conscience. And our conscience, too, is called a law of our mind. Further, the assault of the wicked one, that is the law of sin, settling in the members of our flesh, makes its assault upon us through it. For by once voluntarily transgressing the law of God and receiving the assault of the wicked one, we gave entrance to it, being sold by ourselves to sin. Wherefore our body is readily impelled to it. And so the savour and perception of sin that is stored up in our body, that is to say, lust and pleasure of the body, is law in the members of our flesh.

Therefore the law of my mind, that is, the conscience, sympathises with the law of God, that is, the precept, and makes that its will. But the law of sin , that is to say, the assault made through the law that is in our members, or through the lust and inclination and movement of the body and of the irrational part of the soul, is in opposition to the law of my mind, that is to conscience, and takes me captive (even though I make the law of God my will and set my love on it, and make not sin my will), by reason of commixture : and through the softness of pleasure and the lust of the body and of the irrational part of the soul, as I said, it leads me astray and induces me to become the servant of sin. But *what the law could not do, in that it was weak through the flesh, God, sending His own Son in the likeness of sinful flesh* (for He assumed flesh but not sin) *condemned sin in the flesh, that the righteousness of the law might be fulfilled in us who walk not after the flesh but in the Spirit* Romans 8:3-4 . *For the Spirit helps our infirmities* and affords power to the law of our mind, against the law that is in our members. For the verse, *we know not what we should pray for as we ought, but the Spirit itself makes intercession with groanings that cannot be uttered* , itself teaches us what to pray for. Hence it is impossible to carry out the precepts of the Lord except by patience and prayer.

Chapter 23. Against the Jews on the question of the Sabbath.

The seventh day is called the Sabbath and signifies rest. For in it God rested from all His works Genesis 2:2, as the divine Scripture says: and so the number of the days goes up to seven and then circles back again and begins at the first. This is the precious number with the Jews, God having ordained that it should be held in honour, and that in no chance fashion but with the imposition of most heavy penalties for the transgression. And it was not in a simple fashion that He ordained this, but for certain reasons understood mystically by the spiritual and clear-sighted.

So far, indeed, as I in my ignorance know, to begin with inferior and more dense things, God, knowing the denseness of the Israelites and their carnal love and propensity towards matter in everything, made this law: first, in order that *the servant and the cattle should rest* Deuteronomy 5:14 as it is written, for *the righteous man regards the life of his beast* Proverbs 12:10: next, in order that when they take their ease from the distraction of material things, they may gather together unto God, spending the whole of the seventh day in psalms and hymns and spiritual songs and the study of the divine Scriptures and resting in God. For when the law did not exist and there was no divinely-inspired Scripture, the Sabbath was not consecrated to God. But when the divinely-inspired Scripture was given by Moses, the Sabbath was consecrated to God in order that on it they, who do not dedicate their whole life to God, and who do not make their desire subservient to the Master as though to a Father, but are like foolish servants, may on that day talk much concerning the exercise of it, and may abstract a small, truly a most insignificant, portion of their life for the service of God, and this from fear of the chastisements and punishments which threaten transgressors. *For the law is not made for a righteous man but for the unrighteous.* 1 Timothy 1:9 Moses, of a truth, was the first to abide fasting with God for forty days and again for another forty , and thus doubtless to afflict himself with hunger on the Sabbaths although the law forbade self-affliction on the Sabbath. But if they should object that this took place before the law, what will they say about Elias the Thesbite who accomplished a journey of forty days on one meal 1 Kings 19:8? For he, by thus afflicting himself on the Sabbaths not only with hunger but with the forty days' journeying, broke the Sabbath: and yet God, Who gave the law, was not angry with him but showed Himself to him on Choreb as a reward for his virtue. And what will they say about Daniel? Did he not spend three weeks without food Daniel 10:2? And again, did not all Israel circumcise the child on the Sabbath, if it happened to be the eighth day after birth Genesis 17:12? And do they not hold the great fast which the law enjoins if it falls on the Sabbath Leviticus 16:31? And further, do not the priests and the Levites profane the Sabbath in the works of the tabernacle Matthew 12:5 and yet are held blameless? Yea, if an ox should fall into a pit on the Sabbath, he who draws it forth is blameless, while he who neglects to do so is condemned. And did not all the Israelites compass the walls of Jericho bearing the Ark of God for seven days, in which assuredly the Sabbath was included Joshua iii .

As I said , therefore, for the purpose of securing leisure to worship God in order that they might, both servant and beast of burden, devote a very small share to Him and be at rest, the observance of the Sabbath was devised for the carnal that were still childish and *in the bonds of the elements of the world* Galatians 4:3, and unable to conceive of anything beyond the body and the letter. *But when the fullness of the time had come, God sent forth His Only-begotten Son, made of a woman, made under the law, to redeem them that were under the law that we might receive the adoption of sons. For to as many of us as received Him, He gave power to become sons of God, even to them that believe in Him* John 1:12 . *So that we are no longer servants but sons* Galatians 4:7: no longer under the law but under grace: no longer do we serve God in part from fear, but we are bound to dedicate to Him the whole span of our life, and cause that servant, I mean wrath and desire, to cease from sin and bid it devote itself to the service of God, always directing our whole desire towards God and arming our wrath against the enemies of God: and likewise we hinder that beast of burden, that is the body, from the servitude of sin, and urge it forwards to assist to the uttermost the divine precepts.

These are the things which the spiritual law of Christ enjoins on us and those who observe that become superior to the law of Moses. *For when that which is perfect has come, then that which is in part shall be done away* 1 Corinthians 13:10: and when the covering of the law, that is, the veil, is rent asunder through the crucifixion of the Saviour, and the Spirit shines forth with tongues of fire, the letter shall be done away with, bodily things shall come to an end, the law of servitude shall be fulfilled, and the law of liberty be bestowed on us. Yea we shall celebrate the perfect rest of human nature, I mean the day after the resurrection, on which the Lord Jesus, the Author of Life and our Saviour, shall lead us into the heritage promised to those who serve God in the spirit, a heritage into which He entered Himself as our forerunner after He rose from the dead, and whereon, the gates of Heaven being opened to Him, He took His seat in bodily form at the right hand of the Father, where those who keep the spiritual law shall also come.

What belongs to us , therefore, who walk by the spirit and not by the letter, is the complete abandonment of carnal things, the spiritual service and communion with God. For circumcision is the abandonment of carnal pleasure and of whatever is superfluous and unnecessary. For the foreskin is nothing else than the skin which it superfluous to the organ of lust. And, indeed, every pleasure which does not arise from God nor is in God is superfluous to pleasure: and of that the foreskin is the type. The Sabbath, moreover, is the cessation from sin; so that both things happen to be one, and so both together, when observed by those who are spiritual, do not bring about any breach of the law at all.

Further, observe that the number seven denotes all the present time, as the most wise Solomon says, to give a portion to seven and also to eight. Ecclesiastes 11:2 And David , the divine singer when he composed the eighth psalm, sang of the future restoration after the resurrection from the dead. Since the Law, therefore, enjoined that the seventh day should be spent in rest from carnal things and devoted to spiritual things, it was a mystic indication to the true Israelite who had a mind to see God, that he should through all time offer himself to God and rise higher than carnal things.

Chapter 24. Concerning Virginity.

Carnal men abuse virginity , and the pleasure-loving bring forward the following verse in proof, *Cursed be every one that raises not up seed in Israel.* But we, made confident by God the Word that was made flesh of the Virgin, answer that virginity was implanted in man's nature from above and in the beginning. For man was formed of virgin soil. From Adam alone was Eve created. In Paradise virginity held sway. Indeed, Divine Scripture tells that *both Adam and Eve were naked and were not ashamed.* Genesis 2:23 But after their transgression they knew that they were naked, and in their shame they sewed aprons for themselves. And when, after the transgression, Adam heard, *dust you are and unto dust shall you return* , when death entered into the world by reason of the transgression, then *Adam knew Eve his wife, and she conceived and bare seed.* Genesis 4:1 So that to prevent the wearing out and destruction of the race by death, marriage was devised that the race of men may be preserved through the procreation of children.

But they will perhaps ask, what then is the meaning of male and female Genesis 1:27, and Be fruitful and multiply? In answer we shall say that Be fruitful and multiply does not altogether refer to the multiplying by the marriage connection. For God had power to multiply the race also in different ways, if they kept the precept unbroken to the end. But God, Who knows all things before they have existence, knowing in His foreknowledge that they would fall into transgression in the future and be condemned to death, anticipated this and made male and female, and bade them be fruitful and multiply. Let us, then, proceed on our way and see the glories of virginity: and this also includes chastity.

Noah when he was commanded to enter the ark and was entrusted with the preservation of the seed of the world received this command, *Go in*, says the Lord, *you and your sons, and your wife, and your sons' wives*. He separated them from their wives in order that with purity they might escape the flood and that shipwreck of the whole world. After the cessation of the flood, however, He said, *Go forth of the ark, you and your sons, and your wife, and your sons' wives*. Genesis 8:16 Lo, again, marriage is granted for the sake of the multiplication of the race. Next, Elias, the fire-breathing charioteer and sojourner in heaven did not embrace celibacy, and yet was not his virtue attested by his super-human ascension 2 Kings 2:11? Who closed the heavens? Who raised the dead ? Who divided Jordan ? Was it not the virginal Elias? And did not Elisha, his disciple, after he had given proof of equal virtue, ask and obtain as an inheritance a double portion of the grace of the Spirit ? What of the three youths? Did they not by practising virginity become mightier than fire, their bodies through virginity being made proof against the fire Daniel 3:20? And was it not Daniel's body that was so hardened by virginity that the wild beasts' teeth could not fasten in it. Did not God, when He wished the Israelites to see Him, bid them purify the body ? Did not the priests purify themselves and so approach the temple's shrine and offer victims? And did not the law call chastity the great vow?

The precept of the law, therefore, is to be taken in a more spiritual sense. For there is spiritual seed which is conceived through the love and fear of God in the spiritual womb, travailing and bringing forth the spirit of salvation. And in this sense must be understood this verse: *Blessed is he who has seed in Zion and posterity in Jerusalem*. For does it mean that, although he be a whoremonger and a drunkard and an idolater, he is still blessed if only he has seed in Sion and posterity in Jerusalem? No one in his senses will say this.

Virginity is the rule of life among the angels, the property of all incorporeal nature. This we say without speaking ill of marriage: God forbid! (for we know that the Lord blessed marriage by His presence John 2:1, and we know him who said, *Marriage is honourable and the bed undefiled* Hebrews 13:4), but knowing that virginity is better than marriage, however good. For among the virtues, equally as among the vices, there are higher and lower grades. We know that all mortals after the first parents of the race are the offspring of marriage. For the first parents were the work of virginity and not of marriage. But celibacy is, as we said, an imitation of the angels. Wherefore virginity is as much more honourable than marriage, as the angel is higher than man. But why do I say angel? Christ Himself is the glory of virginity, who was not only-begotten of the Father without beginning or emission or connection, but also became man in our image, being made flesh for our sakes of the Virgin without connection, and manifesting in Himself the true and perfect virginity. Wherefore, although He did not enjoin that on us by law (for as He said, *all men cannot receive this saying* Matthew 19:11), yet in actual fact He taught us that and gave us strength for it. For it is surely clear to every one that virginity now is flourishing among men.

Good indeed is the procreation of children enjoined by the law, and good is marriage on account of fornications, for it does away with these 1 Corinthians 7:2, and by lawful intercourse does not permit the madness of desire to be enflamed into unlawful acts. Good is marriage for those who have no continence: but that virginity is better which increases the fruitfulness of the soul and offers to God the seasonable fruit of prayer. *Marriage is honourable and the bed undefiled, but whoremongers and adulterers God will judge* Hebrews 13:4 .

Chapter 25. Concerning the Circumcision.

The Circumcision was given to Abraham before the law, after the blessings, after the promise, as a sign separating him and his offspring and his household from the Gentiles with whom he lived. Genesis 17:10 And this is evident , for when the Israelites passed forty years alone by themselves in the desert, having no intercourse with any other race, all that were born in the desert were uncircumcised: but when Joshua led them across Jordan, they were circumcised, and a second law of circumcision was instituted. For in Abraham's time the law of circumcision was given, and for the forty years in the desert it fell into abeyance. And again for the second time God gave the law of Circumcision to Joshua, after the crossing of Jordan, according as it is written in the book of Joshua, the son of Nun: *At that time the Lord said to Joshua, Make you knives of stone from the sharp rock, and assemble and circumcise the sons of Israel a second time* Joshua 5:2; and a little later: *For the children of Israel walked forty and two years in the wilderness of Battaris , till all the people that were men of war, which came out of Egypt, were uncircumcised, because they obeyed not the voice of the Lord: unto whom the Lord swore that He would not show them the good land, which the Lord swore unto their fathers that He would give them, a land that flows with milk and honey. And their children, whom He raised up in their stead, them Joshua circumcised: for they were uncircumcised, because they had not circumcised them by the way.* Joshua 5:6-7 So that the circumcision was a sign, dividing Israel from the Gentiles with whom they dwelt.

It was, moreover, a figure of baptism. For just as the circumcision does not cut off a useful member of the body but only a useless superfluity, so by the holy baptism we are circumcised from sin, and sin clearly is, so to speak, the superfluous part of desire and not useful desire. For it is quite impossible that any one should have no desire at all nor ever experience the taste of pleasure. But the useless part of pleasure, that is to say, useless desire and pleasure, it is this that is sin from which holy baptism circumcises us, giving us as a token the precious cross on the brow, not to divide us from the Gentiles (for all the nations received baptism and were sealed with the sign of the Cross), but to distinguish in each nation the faithful from the faithless. Wherefore, when the truth is revealed, circumcision is a senseless figure and shade. So circumcision is now superfluous and contrary to holy baptism. *For he who is circumcised is a debtor to do the whole law.* Galatians 5:3 Further, the Lord was circumcised that He might fulfil the law: and He fulfilled the whole law and observed the Sabbath that He might fulfil and establish the law. Matthew 5:17 Moreover after He was baptized and the Holy Spirit had appeared to men, descending on Him in the form of a dove, from that time the spiritual service and conduct of life and the Kingdom of Heaven was preached.

Chapter 26. Concerning the Antichrist.

It should be known that the Antichrist is bound to come. Every one, therefore, who confesses not that the Son of God came in the flesh and is perfect God and became perfect man, after being God, is Antichrist. 1 John 2:22 But in a peculiar and special sense he who comes at the consummation of the age is called Antichrist. First, then, it is requisite that the Gospel should be preached among all nations, as the Lord said Matthew 24:14, and then he will come to refute the impious Jews. For the Lord said to them: *I have come in My Father's name and you receive Me not: if another shall come in his own name, him you will receive.* John 5:43 And the apostle says, *Because they received not the love of the truth that they might be saved, for this cause God shall send them a strong delusion that they should believe a lie: that they all might be damned who believed not the truth, but had pleasure in unrighteousness.* The Jews accordingly did not receive the Lord Jesus Christ who was the Son of God and God, but receive the impostor who calls himself God. For that he will assume the name of God, the angel teaches Daniel, saying these words, *Neither shall he regard the God of his fathers.* Daniel 11:37 And the apostle says: *Let no man deceive you by any means: for that day shall not come except there come a falling away first, and that man of sin be revealed, the son of perdition: who opposes and exalts himself above all that is called God or that is worshipped, so that he sits in the temple of God* 2 Thessalonians 2:3-4 *, showing himself that he is God;* in the temple of God he said; not our temple, but the old Jewish temple. For he will come not to us but to the Jews: not for Christ or the things of Christ: wherefore he is called Antichrist.

First, therefore, it is necessary that the Gospel should be preached among all nations Matthew 25:14: *And then shall that wicked one be revealed, even him whose coming is after the working of Satan with all power and signs and lying wonders , with all deceivableness of unrighteousness in them that perish, whom the Lord shall consume with the word of His mouth and shall destroy with the brightness of His coming.* The devil himself , therefore does not become man in the way that the Lord was made man. God forbid! But he becomes man as the offspring of fornication and receives all the energy of Satan. For God, foreknowing the strangeness of the choice that he would make, allows the devil to take up his abode in him.

He is, therefore, as we said, the offspring of fornication and is nurtured in secret, and on a sudden he rises up and rebels and assumes rule. And in the beginning of his rule, or rather tyranny, he assumes the role of sanctity. But when he becomes master he persecutes the Church of God and displays all his wickedness. But he will come *with signs and lying wonders* 2 Thessalonians 2:9, fictitious and not real, and he will deceive and lead away from the living God those whose mind rests on an unsound and unstable foundation, so that even the elect shall, if it be possible, be made to stumble Matthew 24:24 .

But Enoch and Elias the Thesbite shall be sent and shall turn the hearts of the fathers to the children , that is, the synagogue to our Lord Jesus Christ and the preaching of the apostles: and they will be destroyed by him. And the Lord shall come out of heaven, just as the holy apostles beheld Him going into heaven, perfect God and perfect man, with glory and power, and will destroy the man of lawlessness, the son of destruction, with the breath of His mouth. Acts 1:11 Let no one, therefore, look for the Lord to come from earth, but out of Heaven, as He himself has made sure 2 Thessalonians 2:8 .

Chapter 27. Concerning the Resurrection.

We believe also in the resurrection of the dead. For there will be in truth, there will be, a resurrection of the dead, and by resurrection we mean resurrection of bodies. 1 Corinthians 15:35-44 For resurrection is the second state of that which has fallen. For the souls are immortal, and hence how can they rise again? For if they define death as the separation of soul and body, resurrection surely is the re-union of soul and body, and the second state of the living creature that has suffered dissolution and downfall. It is, then, this very body, which is corruptible and liable to dissolution, that will rise again incorruptible. For He, who made it in the beginning of the sand of the earth, does not lack the power to raise it up again after it has been dissolved again and returned to the earth from which it was taken, in accordance with the reversal of the Creator's judgment.

For if there is no resurrection, let us eat and drink : let us pursue a life of pleasure and enjoyment. If there is no resurrection, wherein do we differ from the irrational brutes? If there is no resurrection, let us hold the wild beasts of the field happy who have a life free from sorrow. If there is no resurrection, neither is there any God nor Providence, but all things are driven and borne along of themselves. For observe how we see most righteous men suffering hunger and injustice and receiving no help in the present life, while sinners and unrighteous men abound in riches and every delight. And who in his senses would take this for the work of a righteous judgment or a wise providence? There must be, therefore, there must be, a resurrection. For God is just and is the rewarder of those who submit patiently to Him. Wherefore if it is the soul alone that engages in the contests of virtue, it is also the soul alone that will receive the crown. And if it were the soul alone that revels in pleasures, it would also be the soul alone that would be justly punished. But since the soul does not pursue either virtue or vice separate from the body, both together will obtain that which is their just due.

Nay, the divine Scripture bears witness that there will be a resurrection of the body. God in truth says to Moses after the flood, *Even as the green herb have I given you all things. But flesh with the life thereof, which is the blood thereof, shall you not eat. And surely your blood of your lives will I require; at the hand of every beast will I require it, and at the hand of every man's brother will I require the life of man. Whoever sheds man's blood, for his blood his own shall be shed, for in the image of God made I man.* How will He require the blood of man at the hand of every beast, unless because the bodies of dead men will rise again? For not for man will the beasts die.

And again to Moses, *I am the God of Abra ham, the God of Isaac and the God of Jacob: God is not the God of the dead* (that is, those who are dead and will be no more), *but of the living* , whose souls indeed live in His hand Wisdom 3:1, but whose bodies will again come to life through the resurrection. And David, sire of the Divine, says to God, *You take away their breath, they die and return to their dust.* See how he speaks about bodies. Then he subjoins this, *You send forth Your Spirit, they are created: and You renew the face of the earth.*

Further Isaiah says: *The dead shall rise again, and they that are in the graves shall awake.* Isaiah 26:18 And it is clear that the souls do not lie in the graves, but the bodies.

And again, the blessed Ezekiel says: *And it was as I prophesied, and behold a shaking and the bones came together, bone to his bone, each to its own joint: and when I beheld, lo, the sinews came up upon them and the flesh grew and rose up on them and the skin covered them above.* Ezekiel 37:7 And later he teaches how the spirits came back when they were bidden.

And divine Daniel also says: *And at that time shall Michael stand up, the great prince which stands for the children of your people: and there shall be a time of trouble, such trouble as never was since there was a nation on the earth even to that same time. And at that time your people shall be delivered, every one that shall be found written in the book. And many of them that sleep in the dust of the earth shall awake: some to everlasting life and some to shame and everlasting contempt. And they that be wise shall shine as the brightness of the firmament, and out of the multitude of the just shall shine like stars into the ages and beyond.* The words, *many of them that sleep in the dust of the earth shall awake*, clearly show that there will be a resurrection of bodies. For no one surely would say that the souls sleep in the dust of the earth.

Moreover, even the Lord in the holy Gospels clearly allows that there is a resurrection of the bodies. *For they that are in the graves, He says, shall hear His voice and shall come forth: they that have done good unto the resurrection of life, and they that have done evil unto the resurrection of damnation.* John 5:28-29 Now no one in his senses would ever say that the souls are in the graves.

But it was not only by word, but also by deed, that the Lord revealed the resurrection of the bodies. First He raised up Lazarus, even after he had been dead four days, and was stinking. John 11:39-44 For He did not raise the soul without the body, but the body along with the soul: and not another body but the very one that was corrupt. For how could the resurrection of the dead man have been known or believed if it had not been established by his characteristic properties? But it was in fact to make the divinity of His own nature manifest and to confirm the belief in His own and our resurrection, that He raised up Lazarus who was destined once more to die. And the Lord became Himself the first-fruits of the perfect resurrection that is no longer subject to death. Wherefore also the divine Apostle Paul said: *If the dead rise not, then is not Christ raised. And if Christ be not raised, our faith is vain: we are yet in our sins.* 1 Corinthians 15:16-17 And, *Now is Christ risen from the dead and become the first-fruits of them that slept , and the first-born from the dead* Colossians 1:18; and again, *For if we believe that Jesus died and rose again, even so them also which sleep in Jesus will God bring with Him.* 1 Thessalonians 4:14 *Even so,* he said, *as Christ rose again.* Moreover, that the resurrection of the Lord was the union of uncorrupted body and soul (for it was these that had been divided) is manifest: for He said, *Destroy this temple, and in three days I will raise it up.* John 2:19 And the holy Gospel is a trustworthy witness that He spoke of His own body. *Handle Me and see,* the Lord said to His own disciples when they were thinking that they saw a spirit, *that it is I Myself, and that I am not changed* Luke 24:37 *: for a spirit has not flesh or bones, as you see Me have.* And when He had said this He showed them His hands and His side, and stretched them forward for Thomas to touch. John 20:27 Is not this sufficient to establish belief in the resurrection of bodies?

Again the divine apostle says, *For this corruptible must put on incorruption, and this mortal must put on immortality.* 1 Corinthians 15:35 And again: *It is sown in corruption, it is raised in incorruption: it is sown in weakness, it is raised in power: it is sown in dishonour, it is raised in glory: it is sown a natural body* (that is to say, crass and mortal), *it is raised a spiritual body* 1 Corinthians 15:42, 44, such as was our Lord's body after the resurrection which passed through closed doors, was unwearying, had no need of food, or sleep, or drink. *For they will be,* says the Lord, *as the angels of God* Mark 12:25: there will no longer be marriage nor procreation of children. The divine apostle, in truth, says, *For our conversation is in heaven, from whence also we look for the Saviour, the Lord Jesus, Who shall change our vile body that it may be fashioned like His glorious body* Philippians 3:20-21: not meaning change into another form (God forbid!), but rather the change from corruption into incorruption.

But some one will say, *How are the dead raised up?* Oh, what disbelief! Oh, what folly! Will He, Who at His solitary will changed earth into body, Who commanded the little drop of seed to grow in the mother's womb and become in the end this varied and manifold organ of the body, not the rather raise up again at His solitary will that which was and is dissolved? *And with what body do they come* 1 Corinthians 15:35 *? Thou fool,* if your hardness will not permit you to believe the words of God, at least believe His works. *For that which you sow is not quickened except it die* 1 Corinthians 15:35 . *And that which you sow, you sow not that body that shall be, but bare grain, it may chance of wheat or of some other grain. But God gives it a body as it has pleased Him, and to every seed his own body.* Behold, therefore, how the seed is buried in the furrows as in tombs. Who is it that gives them roots and stalk and leaves and ears and the most delicate beards? Is it not the Maker of the universe? Is it not at the bidding of Him Who has contrived all things? Believe, therefore, in this wise, even that the resurrection of the dead will come to pass at the divine will and sign. For He has power that is able to keep pace with His will.

We shall therefore rise again, our souls being once more united with our bodies, now made incorruptible and having put off corruption, and we shall stand beside the awful judgment-seat of Christ: and the devil and his demons and the man that is his, that is the Antichrist and the impious and the sinful, will be given over to everlasting fire: not material fire like our fire, but such fire as God would know. But those who have done good will shine forth as the sun with the angels into life eternal, with our Lord Jesus Christ, ever seeing Him and being in His sight and deriving unceasing joy from Him, praising Him with the Father and the Holy Spirit throughout the limitless ages of ages. Amen.